The Middle Class Credo: "1000 All American Beliefs?"

By T. L. Brink

Published by
R & E Publishers
P. O. Box 2008
Saratoga, California 95070

Library of Congress Card Catalog Number
82-61479

I.S.B.N.
0-88247-703-X

TABLE OF CONTENTS

Introduction. 1

American Social Class. 3

Bureaucracy 9

Business & Economics 12

Celebrities 15

Characters 18

Children 22

Clothes 27

Communism. 30

Crime 32

Death & Dying 35

Education 36

Etiquette & Parties 39

Fat. 42

Food. 44

Foreigners 47

Hair 51

Health. 53

Humor 58

Language & Literature 60

Marriage & Family. 63

Men & Women 66

Minor Frustrations. 72

Movies. 76

Music 79

Names. 81

Older People. 84

Opinions 87

Pets 89

Places 91

Politics 96

Press. 102

Products 104

Racial Minorities. 108

Recreation & Sports. 111

Religion. 115

Residences 117

Salesmen 119

Science & Technology 120

Sex. 122

Teenagers. 127

Transportation 129

Television & Radio 133

Vices. 136

War. 139

Work. 141

Conclusion. 148

Appendix on Method. 150

References. 154

About the Author. 156

INTRODUCTION

The purpose of this book is not to convince the reader to believe anything new, but to make the reader aware of what is already believed, and perhaps get the reader to re-examine the foundations and consequences of those beliefs. Many of the credos presented are racist, sexist, agist, or classist. Many are in poor taste in that they discuss things openly which everyone knows (or at least assumes) privately and discusses, if at all, only in intimate company. Some credos display improper grammar and word usage, but all are an attempt to portray current American ideology.

This book was initially undertaken as an attempt to update Nathan and Mencken's (1921) classic *The American Credo*. They arranged over four hundred statements (credos) which purported the essential American beliefs. Many were superstitious; a surprising number appear to fit the 1980's; on the whole they are quite humorous. However, the central motive of the authors, at least as they tell it, was not entertainment, but edification. They contended that their work was actually directed to the scholar and hoped that they were pioneers of a new social science research technique which could counteract the American incapacity for insight.

The foundation of Nathan and Mencken's methodology was the assumption that the identification of primary attitudes is the best way to portray the essential person. An attitude is a learned predisposition, or habit, to respond in a given way to social stimuli. Attitudes have three components: *cognitive* (beliefs that certain things are so), *affective* (feelings that certain things are good or bad, right or wrong), and *behavioral* (actions based upon the feelings and beliefs). Neither false and contradictory beliefs nor distorted values are harmful unless they influence actions. Behavior is the test of a credo. A person can be said to adhere to a given credo only insofar as that person behaves *as if* the facts and values expressed in the credo were true.

Most of the credos presented in this book are in the form of generalized statements without qualifiers such as "most" or "frequently." These qualifiers come only with reflection and consideration of the existence (or potential existence) of exceptions to the generalization. When reflection does take place, action may be based on the assumption that the credo

1

holds always, in all cases. What forestalls rigid response patterns is not that people are so reflective, but that they have diverse and contradictory credos; the credo which guides behavior in one case may not be that which guides behavior in a later case. A disadvantage of this inconsistency between credos is that a great deal of personal and national problems are due to essential contradictions about what is believed, desired or attempted. Personal happiness and national progress require credos that are accurate with respect to the facts and appropriate when it comes to value commitments.

My attempt to write an American credo for the 1980's proved most difficult. It was virtually impossible to come up with credos that reflected the great diversity of subcultures in the United States today. While it is true that America in the 1920's was not a homogenous culture, at least people from different subcultures seemed committed to that goal. There were many immigrants and first generation Americans in Nathan's time, but the national philosophy was that the transplanted foreigners should be Americanized, purged of ethnic peculiarity and led to conform to the dominant Anglo-Saxon-Celtic culture as it had developed on this continent.

The American civilization is more heterogenous today. The replacement of the "melting pot" with the "salad bowl" where ethnic heritage is now seen as worthy of preservation, is one force for more potent subcultures. Other factors promoting a more pluralistic American civilization are geographic, generational and occupational differences. Perhaps the people who work in the electronics industry in California have a culture that differs in important respects from people who work in the "smokestack" industries of the Midwest. Perhaps people who take their vacations in campers participate in a subculture vastly different from those who vacation on luxury liners.

The implication of this pluralistic culture is that it is easier to write a set of credos for a subculture in America than for Americans as a whole. It is the contention of this book that the most pervasive social influence on contemporary American beliefs, values and behavior is social class. Each individual participates in various subcultures, each participation being determined by key variables, but social class is the line of cleavage which yields the largest subcultures (Kohn, 1969). Therefore, the decision was made to write a credo for the American middle class.

AMERICAN SOCIAL CLASS

1

... that middle class people are the very backbone of Americanism.

2

... that America is one of the few countries where most working people are middle class.

3

... that the majority of Americans believe that they are middle class.

4

... that the people who collect and recycle materials are middle class.

6

... that Vista and Peace Corps volunteers come from the middle class.

7

... that if middle class people do not save a sizeable portion of their income, they feel that they should be on a budget.

8

... that there should be no social classes based upon heredity; people should be given equal opportunity, and then each person can be judged on the basis of individual accomplishments.

9

... that the rich get richer and the poor get poorer.

10

... that there are two kinds of upper class people: the undeserving who inherited their wealth, and those who can be proud of the fact that they rose by their own efforts.

11

... that the undeserving members of the upper class have the unmitigated arrogance to look down on self-made individuals as "unsophisticated and ill-bred."

12

... that upper class people are better off than middle class people; better off, but *not* better as people.

13

... that middle class people are better off than lower class people; better off *and* better people.

14

... that while middle class men are embarrassed about tattoos, lower class men raise their sleeves or go around shirtless in order to show off muscles and tattoos.

15

... that children running around with snot or food on their faces are lower class; middle class mothers are very meticulous in cleaning their children's faces, and as soon as their children can talk, middle class mothers shame their children for having a dirty face.

16

... that while middle class people pay their utility bills on time, and with a check, lower class people pay in cash, and are frequently late in meeting their payment deadlines.

17

... that middle class people walk around to search for opportunities to enrich themselves, but lower class people walk around in order to show off their clothes or battery powered stereos, or to look for mischief.

18

... that middle class people worry about inadequate insurance coverage, law suits, and mortgage foreclosures, while lower class people worry about getting a cigarette or beer when they are out.

19

... that there is so much opportunity in this country and so much governmental protection against undeserved hardship, that anyone in the lower class deserves to be there.

20

... that lower class people are either lazy or irresponsible, but usually both.

21

... that if they were given a guaranteed annual income, paid in one lump sum on New Year's Day, they would be broke by Valentine's Day.

22

... that lower class people are very class conscious, and that is why they buy expensive beer, so that when they throw the cans away, everyone else will be able to see how much class they have.

23

... that it seems they rarely get motivated to do anything, unless the emotions of sex or aggression are involved.

24

... that if they were to put as much effort into being studious and industrious as they put into trying to look "tough, cool, and with-it," they would no longer be lower class.

American Social Class — Analysis

All societies, human and animal, tend to stratify so that there are distinctions between the members of the society. The most important social distinctions are those which involve the granting of status or deference to persons (Shils, 1959). A class system or structure within a society is the set of relationships which goes along with the distinctions in status. A given social class is an aggregate of similar status persons within a given society.

Are there social classes in America? The question is not whether social classes exist in America, for if the question is phrased like that, it is contingent upon the definition of social class. (By changing around what we mean by "social class," we can change around the answer to the question.) A more relevant question is whether or not *people behave as if there were social classes*, and if so, how? In a singles bar, the first question asked, if it is not, "Do you come here often?", is "What do you do?" The first question some of my fellow students at a private college asked me was, "What does your father do?" The first question class-conscious women ask a new acquaintance is, "What does your husband do?" We often feel uneasy relating to another person for the first time; we do not know how much deference to show, so we search for signs of status: ancestry, education, occupation or wealth.

Nevertheless, there is a key difference between the social class system in America and the rigid class structure which entraps most foreigners in the role of their ancestors. Indeed, Weber (1968) defined a social class as a station *within* which mobility is easy and typical. The class system in America permits individuals greater mobility *between* classes (Sorokin, 1956). Nathan and Mencken (1921) observed this and noted that if had a profound effect on the national character. People living in a society with no interclass mobility at least have the sense of security that their status is assured. They are not obliged to attempt to enter a higher class nor need they fear slipping down into a lower category. Americans are tempted by the possibility of advancing to a higher station and yet simultaneously threatened with the ever present possibility of losing the little status that they started out with. This may account for what appears in these credos to be an American obsession with class.

An individual's position in a given society's class system is determined by the interaction of several different variables: ancestry, occupation, wealth, residence and accomplishment. In America there is a reluctance, almost a revulsion, at the idea of using anything beyond an individual's power to categorize that individual (8). Therefore, in America. it is almost as if individual accomplishments and other aspects of personal behavior are to be taken as *the* criteria for determining class membership. In America, people who think and act middle class, regardless of their ancestry, education, occupation or wealth, are accepted as middle class.

The consensus among sociologists is that there are four social classes in America: upper, middle, working and lower (Lundberg, 1974). In reality, the notion that there are four distinct classes is an artificial attempt to divide people arrayed along a continuum into a finite number of categories. (Often it is not even clear what is the relative position of two individuals on that continuum, let alone their class assignment.) It is especially difficult to distinguish between working class and middle class in America (2). Take the case of an immigrant grocer who owns his own store and earns $35,000 a year, and a new assistant professor of history at a private college who earns less than half that amount. Who has more status? We could argue that either one was working class or middle class. I would classify them both as middle class because both have exemplified an ethic of sacrificing in the present in order to progress in the future. The concept of a broad, inclusive middle class is certainly found in these credos (1-3).

The concept of future orientation as the hallmark of class membership was developed by Banfield (1974). He contended that the time-horizon of each class is directly proportional to its status, and tends to permeate all aspects of their social behavior: child-rearing, consumption, manners, sex and work. The lower class has little awareness of the future, so they are improvident, lazy and careless. They see that events are determined by luck rather than their own sacrifices. Working class, and especially middle class persons have a longer view of things and attach more importance to the long term impact of persent sacrifice or indulgence. Upper class people look even further, beyond their own lifetimes and think about the security and progress of future generations of descendants and fellow citizens. Future orientation as a function of class is reflected in these credos (5-7, 16, 18, 21, 24).

A major psychodynamic underlying much of human behavior is the desire to replace a feeling of inferiority with one of superiority (Adler, 1956). Because the class system deals with differentials of status, it is bound to produce or exacerbate feelings of inferiority in all but the upper class (Shils, 1959). One reaction to inferiority feeling is that the prestige that class membership accords itself tends to be higher than that which other classes accord it. This would explain credos 1 and 6, where the middle class touts its own importance to the nation and world. A second reaction to inferiority feeling is to deny the validity of the criteria by which upper classes enjoy their status (credos 8-12). A third reaction to inferiority feeling is to largely ignore the existence of higher prestige people, and focus on those lower in the social order, exaggerating the differences between lower and middle class in order to make the middle class gain a sham sense of superiority. After credo 12, the quantity of credos that refer to the upper class can be counted on one hand. This is because middle class people spend more time thinking about how much better off they are than the lower class, and very little time thinking about how much better off the upper class is. Deprecation of the lower class' cleanliness, morals or responsibility is the central theme of the majority of credos in this section.

What is the recourse of the members of the lower class? They have no one to look down upon. The only solution is to concoct some other bases upon which they can claim superiority, whether it be muscles and tattoos (14) or a "tough, cool, with-it, *baaad* look" (24). In the last century, Veblen (1899) spoke of the new rich as attempting to establish their status by conspicuous consumption. Today it is the lower class which desperately searches for a way to establish a higher status for its members.

It has become the new leisure class, subject to prestige suggestion, and bent on conspicuous consumption (22).

BUREAUCRACY

25
... that a public servant is a bureaucrat if you do not like him.

26
... that in dealing with any large organization, it pays to know someone in a position of power in that organization.

27
... that in any public project, the primary goal is to keep people on the government payroll.

28
... that whenever there is a long line at a government office, some of the workers are at their desks, avoiding the gaze of the crowd, and engaged in shuffling papers or endless phone conversations.

29
... that if we don't pay government workers enough money, they will become susceptible to graft and corruption.

30
... that government workers are better paid than their counterparts in private industry.

31
... that the bureaucrats have planned more aspects of our lives than we can even begin to imagine.

33
... that federal regulations result in a lot of paperwork, but rarely solve the problem.

34
... that no one ever checks the information on government forms as long as you put something in each box.

35
... that phone numbers of government agencies are usually classified in such a way that it is most difficult to find them in the phone book.

36
... that the lawn sprinklers around public buildings go on and off automatically, whether or not it is raining.

37
... that the cost of a first class stamp is outrageous, but most people do not complain to their letter carriers for fear of poorer service.

38
... that the postal service is the only business where the customer is always wrong.

39
... that the mail is so inefficient nowadays because the government had to hire all of those minorities who could not read or write.

40
... that very few people find their jobs through the state department of employment.

41
... that the primary way which this department fights unemployment is by providing jobs to several thousand bureaucrats.

42
... that the Internal Revenue Service bullies small fry in order to set an example.

43
... that people under 40 will never get back from Social Security as much as they put in.

44
... that Social Security is going bankrupt unless something is done.

45

. . . that we can't tinker with Social Security because that would be unfair to the millions of workers who have already paid into it.

46

. . . that no one knows, at any given point, exactly what the national debt is.

47

. . . that there is a lot of waste in the department of . . .

Bureaucracy — Analysis

Bureaucracy is very unpopular among the American middle class, which fails to accept the conclusion of most industrial sociologists: that there are certain conditions under which bureaucracy's standardization of work processes is the most appropriate organizational structure for meeting goals (Mintzberg, 1979). The middle class frustration with bureaucracy is due to several factors. One is that the apparent inefficiency of bureaucracy (28, 33, 35-36, 47) goes against the middle class ethic of scrimping and saving. A second is that bureaucracy does not lend itself to rapid advancement through personal achievement. Most bureaucrats are clearly middle class people, but the salaries, benefits, and job security they enjoy are considered unearned and unjustified by other middle class people. Third, the bureaucracy is perceived as existing in order to provide services for the lower class (27, 41) and these are seen as undeserved. Fourth, middle class people are accorded little deference by bureaucracies (26,38). Fifth, bureaucrats interfere in individual lives through control and fear, and frustrate personal achievements (32, 37, 42).

BUSINESS & ECONOMICS

48

... that most of the stuff they teach about organizations in colleges and schools of business administration just does not apply in this case.

49

... that the larger the corporation, the less it cares about the impact of its decisions on the community.

50

... that the larger the corporation, the more it cares about its public image.

51

... that corporations are undertaxed.

52

... that the double taxation on dividends stifles investment.

53

... that when the pump price of gasoline doubled in America, the world-wide energy crisis became a worldwide glut of oil.

54

... that people who have their automobiles repossessed think that the finance companies are cruel and that there ought to be a law against that sort of thing.

55

... that if the price of something is high, some middleman is making a bundle.

56

... that the fellow who invented pet rocks got rich quick.

57

... that anyone who develops a variant on the chain letter gets rich quick.

58

... that fast food franchises are highly profitable.

59

... that most small restaurants do not make a profit.

60

... that no one reads both sides of a credit card agreement before signing.

61

... that if people had to make all of their purchases in cash, they would make fewer purchases.

62

... that the best investment is the one that went up most last year.

63

... that if you could accurately predict the direction and duration of any fad, you could make a fortune in the stock market.

64

... that an account in a Swiss bank is very safe.

65

... that life insurance does not give as good a financial return as most other investments.

66

... that it is a lot tougher today, economically, for the average American family than it was 15 years ago.

67

... that inflation will get worse.

Business & Economics — Analysis

Level of income is an important factor for membership in a social class (Coleman & Rainwater, 1978). The economic position of the middle class has deteriorated over the past 15 years (66-67) such that many lower-paying college educated and supposedly middle class occupations have lower incomes than some traditionally lower class occupations (Rothman, 1978). As a result, many middle class persons have developed a resentment of the wealth that entrepreneurs and wise investors have made, and this is reflected in anti-business attitudes (49-51, 53, 55-57, 63). The resentment is greatest toward the perquisites of the top executives and the tax advantages of the large investors: depreciation, depletion and even business expenses are seen as "loopholes." On the other hand, middle class small investors are frustrated with the small rate of return they can get (52, 59, 62, 65).

CELEBRITIES

68
... that people who talk about celebrities all day long are talking about the most interesting thing in their repertoire.

69
... that most contemporary celebrities are not very interesting to listen to on a talk show.

70
.. that after a person dies, the media's eulogies are so rosy that one would think that the person never did anything bad.

71
... that all actors, musicians, writers, artists, and comedians are somewhat crazy.

72
... that the ones who become very successful, invest their money wisely, are generous with charities, and stay married for 40 years to the same spouse are exceptions to the above.

73
... that old entertainers either die broke or else owning half of southern California.

74
... that any woman who sleeps with a celebrity hopes to conceive a child by him, and even if the child is conceived by someone else, she will initiate a paternity suit against the celebrity; but her motive is not the prospect of monetary gain, it is the notoriety of having slept with the celebrity.

75
... that Shirley Temple was the best child actor/actress in history.

... that Jayne Mansfield was a dumb blond.

... that Mae West and Dolly Parton appeared to be the prototype of the dumb blond, but whether or not they were natural blonds, they were not dumb.

... that Will Rogers never met a man he didn't like.

... that Picasso laughed all the way to the bank.

... that Marilyn Monroe had an affair with ...

... that Elizabeth Taylor has been married to ...

... that with actresses like Brooke Shields and Bo Derek, talent is skin deep.

... that Brooke Shields' mother would have stopped at nothing to make her daughter famous.

... that Jackie Kennedy showed her true colors when she married Onassis.

... that the Kennedy family receives too much press coverage.

... that Joe Namath scored often, on and off the field.

... that Johnny Weismuller was the best Tarzan.

88

... that Charles Lindbergh was braver than the astronauts.

89

... that everyone likes the muppets.

90

... that Charles Bronson is handsomer today than he was 20 years ago.

91

... that Nancy Reagan has had a facelift.

Celebrities — Analysis

Middle class people feel an ambivalence toward celebrities, the former love the fame and fortune of the latter, yet are also resentful that it was (seemingly) attained so easily. Celebrities are a painful reminder that luck, a pretty face, and connections are important. Many middle class people resent the fact that they have worked harder and sacrificed more than celebrities, and yet have so much less to show for it. That is why scandalous news stories are so popular when they deprecate the talent of celebrities (69-71, 76, 82, 84, 91) or cast aspersions that fame and fortune were only payments for sexual favors (74, 80-81, 83, 86). The only celebrities who are beyond middle class contempt are those who share the middle class virtues of marital fidelity, hard work, and thrift (72-73).

CHARACTERS

92

... that most non-conformists attempt to look, think and act like other non-conformists.

93

... that a stranger who is too friendly has an angle.

94

... that beggers who tell you they need money can give you a convincing reason why they need it, but after they get it they do not use it for that reason.

95

... that people who walk around with open mouths are gullible.

96

... that people who say "there are two kinds of people in the world ..." always classify themselves favorably.

97

... that the fellow who got an A on the chemistry test in high school had thick glasses and a poor complexion.

98

... that the people who live around airports complain about the noise, even when the airport was there before they bought their house.

99

... that some people are accident prone, and they tend to be careless in many areas of life and very rough on equipment.

100

... that people who jaywalk in the middle of traffic do not feel the slightest bit embarrassed if they hold up traffic.

101
... that none of the old school friends or army buddies make an effort to stay close, except when they come into town on a trip and are looking for a free meal or lodging.

102
... that most of the people who protest the killing of whales eat meat.

103
... that the people going down the street on roller skates will be doing something else a year from now.

104
... that people get into the Guinness book of world records by doing something ridiculous, and these are the same people who could not make a world record by doing anything serious.

105
... that geniuses border on insanity.

106
... that people with short, quick gestures are self-centered.

107
... that the people who are most prone to lashing out with verbal insults are those who are most vulnerable to the verbal insults of others.

108
... that people who threaten suicide want attention, and those who stand out on the ledge of a city building purposely wait for rush hour so they will have a larger audience.

109
... that people who blink too often suffer from a lack of self-confidence or some neurological disorder.

110
... that children born with cleft palate or harelip have a great desire to succeed.

... that people who were paralyzed very young develop pleasant personalities, while those who were paralyzed after puberty stay mad at the world for two years; then they either get their lives together and become very inspirational or they stay feeling sorry for themselves and become drug addicts.

... that people with dandruff lack social skills, and people with bad breath have even fewer social skills.

... that people who say "I've got my act together now" don't.

... that people who have been through est are afraid that they will look like fools if they admit that they spent several hundred dollars on something that was a waste of time.

... that people who have been through est always have a glib, but irrelevant response for any demand that they cannot deal with.

Characters — Analysis

The more an individual gains a feeling of prestige from social class identification, the more that person is threatened by others who attempt to gain prestige in some other way. Therefore, the Middle Class Credo contains deprecations not only of lower class and upper class people, but also of people who attempt to gain status outside of the class system: celebrities, non-conformists (92), political activists (102), est "graduates" (114-115). Strangers also come in for criticism (93) because their social class is not immediately apparent. Many of the characters identified in this section do not behave according to middle class norms: beggars (94), freeloaders (101), suicide attempters (109) or people who lack a future orientation (98).

However, most of the characters mentioned do not offer a threat to middle class norms, they are just people whom we find aggravating in some way. Several of the credos (97, 104-105, 113) demonstrate some of the envy that is shown to celebrities, the reassurance that other people's advantages are accompanied by disadvantages.

CHILDREN

116
... that even today most babies are the result of unplanned pregnancies.

117
... that expectant fathers are less nervous if they are in the delivery room than the waiting room.

118
... that any child born when the youngest sibling is over age 7 was a late life accident, but the parents will hail the child as a miraculous answer to their prayers, and such children end up very spoiled.

119
... that adopted children will want to know who their biological parents were, especially the mother.

120
... that parents who adopt children feel rejected if the children express an interest in "my real mother."

121
... that people who have given a baby up for adoption do not want to have the child look for them 20 years later.

122
... since abortion has been legalized, it is hard to find a blond, blue-eyed, healthy baby girl up for adoption.

123
... that it is more acceptable for a white couple to adopt an Asian child than a Black child.

... that when a baby stops crying after we pick it up, this is because we have a special way with babies, but when the baby continues to cry after we pick it up, this is because the baby was hungry or in pain.

... that 90% of parents contend that their babies develop faster than average.

... that grandchildren under 5 are more fun than grandchildren over 12.

... that children have an irresistable temptation to write on walls with crayons.

... that the first piece of pottery children make is an ashtray.

... that two year olds have an innate fear of, yet fascination with, the idea of falling back into the toilet and being flushed away.

... that children's parties are especially stressful for the parents of the child hosting the party.

... that when a pair of 12 year old girls rings the doorbell, they are either trying to sell cookies or looking for a lost puppy.

... that after children return home on Halloween, middle class parents carefully examine all the candy.

... that a child will take better care of something if he had to work and save for it.

... that it is unfair to praise a child too strongly when another is close.

... that next to college, the most expensive thing that middle class parents buy their children is braces.

136

... that parenting has always been a hobby, rather than a vocation, for men and it is becoming a hobby, rather than a vocation, for women.

137

... that parents think their children are smarter than the tests indicate, and know that the kids could get better grades if they were to apply themselves.

138

... that kids are not too excited about any holiday where they do not get presents or a day off from school.

139

... that it is one of the great emotional shocks of childhood to be told that there is no Santa Claus.

140

... that it is very hard to get the children of today to believe in Santa Claus.

141

... that children can never wait for Christmas.

142

... that it is extremely difficult to find neighbors whose children are exemplary.

143

... that people blame the incorrigibility of children on the parents, and parents blame peer influence for the incorrigibility of their kids.

144

... that there is less corporal punishment today.

145

... that there is more child abuse today.

146

... that middle class parents scold their kids too much, but discipline them too little, and lower class parents scold their kids too much, and hit them often, but also fail to provide consistent discipline.

147

... that parents are afraid to hit their kids in public for fear of what other people will think.

148

... that the kids are wise to this and get away with a lot more in public than they would even try in the house.

149

... that a merchant is afraid to tell customers how obnoxious their children are.

150

... that the quickest way to silence a demanding child is to give it what it wants, but this is also the best way to insure that the child will be demanding in the future.

151

... that children of today are so grown up for their age.

152

... that children of today are so immature and irresponsible.

153

... that children of today would be better off with twice as much time with their parents and half as many toys; with twice as many chores and half as much freedom.

Children — Analysis

Parenthood is a role which most people, even middle class people, have not adequately prepared themselves for (116, 118, 136). Nevertheless, middle class parents feel an obligation to be responsible parents (132, 135). They hope to become proud of their children (125, 137, 143) and greatly fear both failure and rejection (124, 126).

Children do not inherit the social class consciousness of the parents. Only many years of training can get them to think like middle class adults. The inculcation of middle class values and deportment in their children is the sacred duty of all middle class parents and requires strictness (133, 150, 153). Until the process of inculcation is completed, children can be expected to behave improvidently, lazily and carelessly (127-128, 148).

One prediction for the 1980's is that parenting will become a more significant role and will bestow more status, especially among the middle class. The large cohort known as the "baby boom" generation, born 1945-1955, has grown through its extended adolescence, settled into careers, and is ready to have dignified little middle class families.

CLOTHES

154
... that most new hair and clothes fashions are extreme and unattractive.

155
... that women do not look attractive in baggy jeans, army fatigues, overalls, backpacks, hiking books or bathing caps.

156
... that any woman can get more attention from men with a lower neckline.

157
... that most people wear what fashion dictates rather than what looks best on them; when skirts are high, many homely legs will be seen.

158
... that women who have a hobby of collecting antiques dress frightfully.

159
... that ministers' wives have a wardrobe that is about five years out of style.

160
... that women who dress plainly have a low self-image.

161
... that women who dress plainly have a good self-image, and do not need to dress up to feel good about themselves.

162
... that women who dress stylishly are attracted to men who dress stylishly, and women who dress plainly are attracted to men who are honest

and sensitive.

163
... that after college age, middle class people do not wear clothes with writing on them.

164
... that the lower class tendency to wear clothes with words stems from deficits in the ability to communicate by other means.

165
... that after college age, middle class people do not have pictures larger than half an inch on their clothes.

166
... that people prefer baby clothes that have cute little animal cartoon figures on them, even though the babies are not impressed by the designs.

167
... that only old men and homosexuals wear suspenders.

168
... that men who wear sleeveless shirts or jackets are lower class.

169
... that middle class men will not take off their shirts no matter how hot it gets unless they are near a designated swimming area.

170
... that lower class men will not wear shorts no matter how warm it is.

171
... that lower class men feel very uncomfortable in a suit, and look it

172
... that middle class parents insist that their children wear a jacket or sweater out of doors unless it is 78 degrees, in which case the children will be asked to bring one along.

173
... that parents insist that their children change their good school clothes before going out to play.

Clothes — Analysis

The attempt to gain status by wearing fashionable clothes is frequently employed by groups without prestige in the society at large (e.g., lower class people and teenagers). The middle class frowns on this attempt to gain prestige (156, 163-165, 168). Nevertheless, middle class people realize that clothes are important in building an impression in others, and in order to avoid appearing old, poor or socially unaware (155, 159-160), most middle class people make an effort to be less conspicuous by going along with fashion (157). Of course, if they can enhance the impression they make on others, so much the better, but exaggeration of fashion is a serious violation of the Middle Class Credo.

The last two credos (172-173) in this section reiterate the theme of responsible parenting. Credo 173 is especially important because it conveys the central middle class credo on fashion: dress for the occasion! It is lower class people who buy T-shirts with large cartoon characters and catchy phrases and then wear them for school, work, shopping, dancing, and fixing the car.

COMMUNISM

174

... that communism is the only political, social or economic system ever invented in the history of the world where the leaders have had to build walls to keep the people from running away.

175

... that communism's greatest failure has been in agriculture.

176

... that most communists and ultra-liberals do not come from lower class backgrounds but were spoiled by middle class or upper class parents; they are not workers but frustrated intellectuals.

177

... that civil liberties are good in principle but in practice radicals abuse them.

178

... that socialism probably does not lead to communism but it does not work any better.

179

... that the ACLU always takes the side of communists and criminals.

Communism - Analysis

Middle class people abhor communism for three reasons. First, it claims to be a movement which will champion the poor and abolish all class privilege. Nothing terrifies the middle class as much as being put in the same social class as lower class people. Second, the image we have of communist countries is that commissars ruin the economy and send the secret police around to terrorize the people. Third, the spokespersons for most radical movements represent middle class norms in no way, shape or form.

CRIME

180
... that most hardened criminals were lower class children who had an unhappy childhood.

181
... that people standing around streetcorners are either waiting for a bus or looking for trouble.

182
... that many people are still taken in by scams and buncos, but the victims of con artists share some of the blame because they were too greedy or gullible.

183
... that there is too much talk about police brutality and the protection of the criminal's rights and too little done about protecting the victims.

184
... that criminals were afraid of the law 30 years ago but not today.

185
... that there should be more prisons and less luxury for prisoners.

186
... that most criminals can never be reformed.

187
... that most crimes are committed by someone out on bail or parole.

188
... that the death penalty deters crime, and is certainly the best way to cut down on the number of repeat offenders.

... that when criminals go on a hunger strike, it is best to let them die; after all it is a form of voluntary capital punishment; but the same liberals who oppose capital punishment want to accede to the prisoner's demands.

... that assassins are more motivated to go after popular presidents and popes.

... that no one steals a car that has less than half a tank of gas.

... that anyone who attempts to buy commercial real estate in Florida with a suitcase full of money is involved in the drug trade.

... that most of the time a fire, burglar or air-raid alarm goes off, people assume that it is a false alarm or a test and ignore it.

... that there are some unwise and unfair laws on the books and some of the best laws are not enforced.

... that today, householders who shoot an intruder have more to fear from the law than the intruder does.

... that politicians talk tough on crime but appoint lenient judges.

... that when a rape victim testifies in court, the defense attorney tries to portray her as a woman of low morals who led the defendant on.

Crime — Analysis

Almost all of these credos reflect the middle class frustration with crime. Crime, at least in those forms of it that occur on the street rather than in the office is largely perpetrated by lower class individuals who desire both material gain and a sense of power over others. Middle class people are also striving very hard for those same goals and have some limited attainments of them but only with a great deal of effort, sacrifice and adherence to the rules of the class system. Nothing is more maddening than to have someone else break the rules and take away what you have worked so hard to get by following the rules.

DEATH & DYING

198
... that much of the medical technology which is designed to prolong life merely prolongs the process of dying.

199
... that people should have a right to die with dignity.

200
... that doctors should not be allowed to play God.

201
... that many people are afraid of being buried alive.

202
... that cremation saves the land for the living.

203
... that people feel morally obligated to honor the request of someone who is dying.

204
... that Forest Lawn cemetery is overdone.

Death & Dying — Analysis

Death comes to all social classes. All are helpless before it. Elaborate funerals and elegant private cemeteries are deprecated (204) because middle class people could not afford something like that.

EDUCATION

205
... that the students of today have more to learn than ever before.

206
... that sex education has been a failure.

207
... that school administrators hope that the valedictorian will say nothing that will be remembered by the time that graduation ceremonies are over.

208
... that most graduates of an 8th grade schoolhouse of 40 years ago had better reading, writing, penmanship, spelling, punctuation and grammar than college graduates today, and if you take away the calculator, better arithmetic.

209
... that college professors are absentminded.

210
... that professors are supposed to maintain the illusion that they know more than the students do.

211
... that when the professor responds to the student by saying, "Now, you have raised a good question," it means that the question was better than the answer the professor is thinking of.

212
... that in large and prestigious universities, professors are busy writing books, going to conventions and supervising their graduate students.

... that no subject is so trivial, irrelevant or boring that somebody in some university has not devoted a lifetime to becoming an expert on it.

214

... that the 1960's hippies who dropped out of college never made anything of themselves, but those who stayed in college and graduated now hold the positions of power in this country.

215

... that the most valuable function of higher education in this country is not that it teaches anything relevant (that cannot be learned elsewhere) but that it attests to the ability of people to discipline themselves to meet deadlines and do what they do not want to do for four years.

216

... that education used to do a pretty good job of separating the wheat from the chaff before the days of grade inflation, Mickey Mouse courses, credit for life experience and ethnic minority quotas.

217

... that there are some colleges so desperate for students that the students flunk in instead of flunk out.

218

... that middle class people have a college education or at least wish they did, and certainly want their children to have one.

219

... that only rich people can afford to send two children to a private college without having the wife go back to work.

220

... that the government or parents owe all American children an education up to the highest level for which they are capable.

221

... that if students have to work their way through college, they make wise choices and study harder.

222

... that streaking in 1974 was ridiculous but it was a welcome change from campus riots and bombings.

223
... that since most colleges have lifted visiting hours in the dorms, panty raids are no longer a fad.

224
... that no university campus is easy to find your way around in.

225
... that liberal arts education is largely irrelevant to important considerations like earning a living.

226
... that students who major in the arts or the humanities do not really want to go to work after graduating.

227
... that most of what was learned in college was forgotten and what was remembered has not been that helpful in later life.

228
... that no one reads all of the books that they save from college.

Education — Analysis

In the past, the middle class has been a staunch supporter of publicly financed higher education for all. The middle class believed that a college education was a stepping stone to career advancement. Because higher education has failed to live up to these claims, middle class disillusionment has developed (215-217, 225, 227-228). The diploma, degree and credential are still important but only because their lack is a stumbling block to career development (214-215); they do not, by themselves, assure career development.

The middle class must still send the children to college and resents the high cost of education (219). The people in higher education come in for deprecation (209-211) because they have concocted and perpetuated the myth that college leads to success and they have done this in order to gain status and job security for themselves.

ETIQUETTE & PARTIES

229
... that if one is not yawning, talking or smiling, one's mouth should be closed.

230
... that everyone belches and farts but to do it in front of others is extremely rude unless of course the person passing the wind was embarrassed by it; in which case it is funny.

231
... that picking one's nose in front of others is rude and regardless of how embarrassed the nosepicker gets, it is never funny.

232
... that a person is downright rude to call during a good TV program.

233
... that no one likes to be kept on hold.

234
... that you don't stop giving gifts to someone who remembers your birthday, you don't stop sending Christmas cards to someone until they miss you one year.

235
... that it is impolite to ask someone how much was paid for something.

236
... that people who tell you how little they paid for something are boasting how clever they are, while people who tell you how much they paid for something are boasting how rich and generous they are (if the item was a luxury) or seeking your sympathy (if the item was a necessity).

. . . that if a household has a telephone, there is no excuse for dropping in unexpectedly.

. . . that a good party begins with a good guest list.

. . . that people who talk with their mouths full receive less dinner invitations.

. . . that female guests should offer to help the hostess with the dishes, but should *not insist* on helping.

. . . that the major topic of conversation at middle class dinner parties is the price of real estate.

. . . that the best way to be a good conversationalist is to smile and nod.

. . . that the people who come to the class reunion were the biggest show-offs in high school and people who were not very popular in school come out for the reunions only if they have been very successful.

. . . that no one wants to attend the class reunion of a spouse.

. . . that it is no longer necessary to follow all the etiquette in the books, but manners shoule be good enough not to offend anyone.

. . . that the dirtiest thing for a dinner guest to do is to offer your domestic help a higher paying job.

Etiquette & Parties — Analysis

Since frontier days, most Americans have regarded too much etiquette and formality to be a holdover from the deference bestowed to nobility (de Toqueville, 1966). Upper class people who attend very formal affairs are perceived as "stuffed shirts." On the other hand, lower class people who directly indulge their instincts without concern for manners or decorum are seen as "uncouth." The middle class standard is based upon reason, mutual respect and the avoidance of both intentional offense and artificiality (245). Above all, the middle class standard embodies the virtues of cleanliness and self-control (229-231, 239). Other virtues are mutual exchange (234) and respect for other people's time (232-233, 237). The most contradictory credos are those which relate to wealth (235-236, 241) which reflect the middle class ambivalence toward discussing wealth: the desire to boast of it while appearing to be modest about it.

FAT

247
... that middle class people feel guilty if they are obese, but lower class people feel deprived if they are skinny.

248
... that most middle class people wish they were more slender.

249
... that fat people are warmer in the winter but uncomfortable in the summer.

250
... that fat people are good swimmers and dancers.

251
... that fat people are to blame for being fat; obesity is the wage of the sins of gluttony and sloth.

252
... that men over 25 who drive loud motorcycles have beer bellies.

253
... that people who give up smoking gain weight.

254
... that no one enjoys being on a diet.

255
... that a diet book will sell more copies if its title includes the name of some wealthy suburb.

256
... that fat is still not "in," but it is not as "out" as it was a decade ago.

Fat — Analysis

Obesity is negatively correlated with social class: lower class people are more frequently fat (247, 252). Because of this, the Middle Class Credo attributes obesity to excessive laziness and instinctual gratification (215). Therefore, middle class people have three reasons for staying slender: health, beauty and the desire to avoid looking lower class (247-248).

There is one moderating factor in the middle class condemnation of obesity: the great number of people born between 1945 and 1955 are rapidly heading for middlescence and their bodies are getting stouter, so obesity will be more difficult to avoid than it was for a nation of adolescents in the 1960's (256).

FOOD

257
... that fruits and vegetables taste better if purchased at a little stand in the country but they are cheaper if purchased in the neighborhood supermarket.

258
... that fresh fruits and vegetables are healthful, especially if grown with tender loving care in a home garden.

259
... that few of the radishes grown in home gardens are ever eaten by the people who grow them.

260
... that yogurt is healthful.

261
... that a diet with too many empty calories is dangerous.

262
... that a great amount of processed sugar will lead to diabetes or cancer.

263
... that eating too much sugar leads to hypoglycemia and a craving for sugar, and eventual addiction.

264
... that greasy foods harden the arteries and make acne worse.

265
... that the vitamins you get in pills are not as nutritious as those which come from fresh foods.

... that food additives cause cancer.

... that drinking water was better 10 years ago.

... that the best beer comes from Germany, Holland, England, Argentina, Mexico, or anywhere but Poland or the United States.

... that no one's favorite vegetable is spinach, no one's favorite fruit is prunes.

... that no one's favorite main course is the hot dog, except for some children at the ballpark.

... that some children believe that hot dogs are made from real dogs.

... that hot dogs were more popular 30 years ago.

... that only children enjoy peanut butter and jelly sandwiches for lunch.

... that a tuna fish sandwich is better to eat than to smell.

... that it is trickier to boil rice than to bake a potato.

... that everyone is particular about how a steak is cooked.

... than an 8 year old's favorite restaurant is a fast food place.

... that never before have Americans gone out for so much food.

... that middle class people in metropolitan areas eat a good many of their meals out unless they have children under age 10.

... that middle class people clip coupons, wait for supermarket sales, and compare unit costs.

... that the people on food stamps have enough money for junk food, soft drinks, cigarettes and pet food.

... the food served at the $100 a plate fund raising dinners is not worth it.

Food — Analysis

In general, lower class food and middle class food is not that different in the United States. The big difference comes in the concerns people have about food. The middle class is much more likely to worry about cost (281-283) and nutritional and health aspects (258, 260, 262-266).

FOREIGNERS

284
... that foreign students more frequently cheat on their examinations and plagiarize term papers.

285
... that foreign airports have dirty restrooms.

286
... that there are some foreign countries where they kidnap children and mutilate them so that they will take in more money as beggars.

287
... that if England did not have all that tradition, history and pageantry, it would be a pretty boring place.

288
... that if you don't have ancestors from Ireland, it is a pretty boring place.

289
... that the French are ungrateful, arrogant and unfriendly, especially when it comes to American tourists.

290
... that Japan has the world's most efficient trains.

291
... that wherever Japanese tourists go, they travel in groups and each one has a camera.

292
... that Asians have a harder time digesting wheat than rice.

293

... that people in India could solve their hunger problem by making hamburgers out of the sacred cows.

294

... that Iranians are not fulfilled in life until they have found a cause which they say they will be martyred for.

295

... that the people in any country east of England and west of China smell bad for two generations.

296

... that the poor people in Mexico are nicer than the poor people in the United States.

297

... that on Sundays, Mexicans dress their children very neatly.

298

... that the children in Mexico are hardworking and respect adults.

299

... that Mexico would be better off putting more people working in factories making things and fewer people out on the streets trying to sell things.

300

... that people who cannot speak English are either tourists or illegal aliens, with the former identified by cameras or backpacks.

301

... that if the tide of illegal immigration continues, along with the reduced white birthrate, whites will be a minority in this country in 50 years time.

302

... that there are more Cubans in Miami than in Havana; there are more Jews in New York City than in Tel Aviv; there are more Puerto Ricans in New York than in San Juan; there are more Poles in Chicago than in Krakow; and soon there will be more Haitians in Florida than in Port-au-Prince.

... that the entire pueblo of Aguililla, Michoacan, in Mexico, is now a ghost town, its entire population having been relocated to Redwood City, California.

304

... that if you go to the country of your ancestors, the people there will love you within the first five minutes, but within half an hour, they will think that you are showing off.

305

... that one of the nice things about the United States sending an astronaut to the moon was that it was something these two-bit countries could never do.

306

... that only an expert knows, at any given point in time, exactly how many nations there are in the world.

307

... that it is foolish for the United States government to "refuse to recognize" other governments.

308

... that the United Nations is a wonderful idea and membership in it should be open to all nations, but the organization has not accomplished very much.

309

... that disarmament would be wonderful but we cannot trust the Soviets to live up to the agreement.

Foreigners — Analysis

Sixty years ago, the most pervasive theme in Nathan and Mencken's (1921) credos was the difference between Americans and foreigners. Americans were uncertain of their identity as a nation and needed to define it by means of contrasts with the established identities of Europeans and third world peoples. Today, most of the credos have some sort of division based upon social class. Americans know who they are in the world, but not where they stand in their own country, and this is being intensified by the inflation and taxes which squeeze living standards.

World War II clearly established America as the world's foremost nation. In the past two decades, this status has paralleled that of the middle class: decline. We might still be ahead of most of the world's countries, but they are certainly advancing faster than we are. So Americans tend to console themselves by saying that despite the new found wealth of the old world and third world, foreigners are not generally the equal of Americans, the former being more dishonest (284), dirty (285, 295, 474), foolish (294), boring (287-288), or brutal (286). Americans know how to do things better (305) and a lot of third world problems could be solved if those people would just do it the American way (293, 299), but if we help them, they are ungrateful (289).

Perhaps the most favorable views are those held toward the Japanese (290-291, 716) who are seen as an entire nation which follows the Middle Class credo. Indeed, one patronizing explanation for Japanese economic success is that they are great imitators. Americans overvalue originality and are too proud to look elsewhere in the world for advice. Especially when it comes to social policy issues, Americans seem to forget that other nations have experienced similar problems, tried certain solutions, and observed successes or failures. Therefore, America rarely profits from the experience of foreign nations. In 1962, the San Francisco Bay Area cities decided to develop a rail transportation system, so they started from scratch, hoping to come up with the world's most modern system. A few years later, Mexico City needed such a system, so they carefully studied the subways in Paris and Tokyo. San Francisco's BART (Bay Area Rapid Transit) has been plagued by political delays, labor unrest and innumerable equipment malfunctions, while Mexico City's Metro is fast, efficient and economical.

Americans have always feared that newly arrived immigrants, whether legal or illegal, were coming in too fast and that they could not be Americanized quickly enough to prevent a downgrading of American civilization. The lower class attitude is that immigrants take jobs away from Americans and compete for welfare dollars. The middle class view is that immigrants are okay if they come to work and behave responsibly, for they will become middle class in time. Indeed, immigration tends to select the most ambition and self-sacrificing people, the "cream of the crop" of the sending country (Brink & Brink, 1978). (The last wave of Cuban immigrants might be an exception to this.) The great middle class fear is that the government is bending over backwards to prevent the middle classification of immigrants: giving them too many free services and promoting bilingualism which will impede their Americanization.

HAIR

310
... that some men look better with a beard, but most do not.

311
... that beards are more common on frisbee players.

312
... that liberated women stop shaving their legs and underarms.

313
... that if a woman has beautiful hair, men will notice her from afar.

314
... that some women look good with short hair, but most look better with longer hair.

315
... that most women wish that they had a slightly lighter color of hair.

316
... that men prefer blonds.

317
... that blond is beautiful unless the roots are two inches dark.

318
... that blonds age more quickly.

319
... that most women who drive sports cars have beautiful, natural looking blond hair, but most women who drive old VW's have very unattractive hair.

320

... that men were wearing longer hair in 1975 than in 1965.

321

... that there were more bald men around 40 years ago.

322

... that leaving hair wet is not good for the scalp or hair.

323

... that blow-dryers are not good for the scalp or the hair.

Hair — Analysis

Hair is no longer the issue it was in 1967. Hair is beautiful, provided it is clean and groomed. An unkempt appearance is to be tolerated in adolescence but after that, it is a statement against middle class values. The punker's attempt to make hair ugly is also a statement against middle class values.

HEALTH

324
... that most things are healthful if used in moderation.

325
... that never before have Americans been so healthy.

326
... that when people get upset, their blood pressure rises.

327
... that obnoxious people cause headaches; stressful situations cause ulcers.

328
... that people who let themselves get angry are less likely to develop physical or mental disorders.

329
... that people who freely express thier feelings must be mentally ill.

330
... that children who wet the bed grow up to be neurotic adults.

331
... that everyone acts a bit crazy once in awhile.

332
... that insane people insist that they are Jesus or Napoleon.

333
... that someone who brags about how much benefit he has gotten from est, Arica, Gestalt, primal scream, encounter and psychoanalysis is probably still pretty mixed up.

334

... that when it comes to whiplash, chiropractors are more helpful than physicians but the chiropractor who is also into nutrition counseling, acupuncture and meditation might try to redesign your entire life.

335

... that middle class people bathe and change their underwear before going to the doctor and if a middle class mother hears that her 12 year old son has been rushed to the emergency room, she worries if he was wearing a clean pair of underwear.

336

... that hospital admission rooms are more interested in a patient's coverage than in the patient's condition.

337

... that Chinese hospitals use acupuncture instead of medical anesthetics.

338

... that nothing can save a patient who has lost the will to live.

339

... that hysterectomy is usually unnecessary and afterward the woman gets fatter, more wrinkled and lower-voiced.

340

... that sugar causes cavities but fluoride toothpaste prevents them.

341

... that middle class people try to brush after meals, avoid snacks and see a dentist twice a year.

342

... that you should never put anything in your ear sharper than your elbow.

343

... that the people who follow the above advice have dirty ears.

344

... that popping acne pimples only makes the disease worse.

345

... that lepers are placed in special colonies because the disease is so contagious.

346

... that all diseases are probably contagious; it is just that they have not yet identified the transmitting organism of some.

347

... that most people receiving disability payments exaggerate the extent to which they are disabled.

348

... that there is an epidemic of hyperactivity in children but it was rare 40 years ago when children had adequate chores and discipline.

349

... that smoking causes cancer: cigarettes cause lung cancer, pipes cause mouth cancer, cigars cause lip cancer.

350

... that using someone else's comb can lead to infectious dandruff.

351

... that circumcision is wise for hygienic reasons.

352

... that people with rheumatism can predict changes in the weather.

353

... that appendicitis was more common in the 1950's.

354

... that many people get heart attacks from shoveling snow.

355

... that PCB's are dangerous.

356

... that reading in poor light causes permanent eye damage.

357

... that children catch cold when they do not dress warmly out of doors.

358

... that vitamin C prevents the common cold or helps build resistance.

359

... that while the parents of the 1950's worried about their kids coming down with polio, parents of the 1980's worry about their kids coming down with VD.

360

... that VD is spread more by high school students than by prostitutes.

361

... that in every Veterans Administration hospital, there is one ward devoted entirely to incurable cases of V.D., but this ward is never discussed in public.

362

... that middle class men will wash their hands if there is another man in the bathroom but lower class men will only wash their hands if they are afraid that their wife or mother will find out that they did not wash their hands after using the bathroom.

363

... that the most dangerous germs are those which develop on unwashed dishes and foods left at room temperature for more than 36 hours.

364

... that any sore or pain which has been around for only a short time will probably cure itself if just left alone.

365

... that any sore or pain which has been around for a long time is probably not too dangerous because it has not led to any serious problems.

366

... that hypochondriacs refuse to believe the two previous statements.

367

... that the two greatest dangers in childhood are breaking one's own neck and putting out someone else's eye.

368
... that lower class people feel stupid if they wear a motorcycle helmet while riding, while middle class people who ride motorcycles feel stupid if they do not wear a helmet.

369
... that on Christmas Day the emergency rooms of hospitals are crowded with children who have hurt themselves playing with new toys and adults who have used electric carving knives.

370
... that most forest fires are caused by cigarettes or campfires.

Health — Analysis

The middle class emphasizes the virtues of self-control, cleanliness and caution. Their health beliefs explain why these virtues make sense. Self-control is the moderation and avoidance of bad habits to prevent abuse of the body (324, 349). Cleanliness is necessary to prevent disease (343, 351). Even the appearance of cleanliness is important (335-336). Accidents are not due to luck but to a lack of caution (340-342, 354-358, 363, 367-370). Middle class people are highly concerned about the fact that lower class people are so dirty and careless because diseases are contagious (345-346, 350, 359-360) and innocent people can be injured by the irresponsible.

There is a great middle class interest in mental health, especially psychophysiologic disorders (326-328, 338, 348). Nevertheless, mental health views are somewhat behind the times (329-332), but not nearly as nineteenth century as those of the lower class. After a dozen years of promises of quick-cure psychotherapy, most of the middle class is quite skeptical of it (333).

HUMOR

371
... that grape jokes and knock knock jokes are not funny.

372
... that Charlie Chaplin was the best comedian the screen has ever seen.

373
... that TV comedy was better in the 1950's.

374
... that Archie Bunker was very funny, and right about 70% of the time.

375
... that in an improvisational comedy routine, the only bits that are funny are those that were carefully rehearsed.

376
... that all impressionists do Jimmy Stewart, John Wayne and Humphrey Bogart, but none do Clark Gable or Clint Eastwood.

377
... that in jokes involving a rabbi and a priest, the priest is always the straight man and the rabbi the top banana, and this is due to the fact that there are more Jewish comedians.

378
... that the funniest comics had sad personal lives.

379
... middle class parents would prefer their children to become garbage collectors rather than political activists or comedians.

Humor — Analysis

The middle class view of contemporary humor is far from positive (371-373, 375-376). Likewise, the view of comdians is unfavorable (378-379). Perhaps this is due to the fact that most contemporary humor is anti-middle class, and only the Jews have really learned to laugh at themselves (377). The most successful comedy show of the 1970's, "All In The Family," was probably so successful because Archie Bunker (374) championed stereotyped workingclass values, while his "meat-head" son-in-law championed stereotyped, radical values in such a way that middle class viewers could feel superior to both.

LANGUAGE & LITERATURE

380
. . . that a letter which initiates contact should not have more than one paragraph commencing with the word, "I".

381
. . . that the opening and closing speeches at conventions are mere formalities and only serve to gratify the speaker.

382
. . . that middle class parents are embarrassed by the "you knows" in their children's speech.

383
. . . that C.B. slanguage was a working class cultural fad.

384
. . . that anyone who has a large vocabulary with a slight foreign accent must be highly educated and intellectual.

385
. . . that anyone who uses a large vocabulary and has a heavy regional American accent is trying to show off, and is actually very insecure.

386
. . . that people from Philadelphia talk as though they have a cold, people from Chicago talk as though they are angry, people from Boston talk as though they believe themselves to be superior, and people from Texas talk as though they were trying to prove how tough they are.

387
. . . that country folk speak slower.

388

... that people in the country and people in the city use different swear words but, in either case, profanity reflects a small vocabulary.

389

... that Latin Americans respond warmly when American tourists try to stumble through Spanish but the French respond with indignation when American tourists try to stumble through their language.

390

... that French Canadians know English but refuse to speak it.

391

... that few people feel obliged to follow the rules of grammar anymore.

392

... that the language would be greatly simplified if the spelling of words would match the way that they are pronounced and the conjugation of all verbs became regular.

393

... that the only objection to these changes would come from English teachers who would fear that a few generations after these changes, no one would be able to understand Shakespeare.

394

... that when professors in the humanities write about anything, they use so many quotations from and allusions to famous authors that it is impossible to follow the main theme of the article.

395

... that if the messages on greeting cards are too long, no one will read them.

396

... that lower class people do not read anything more difficult than a comic book after leaving high school.

397

... that Charles Dickens had a fixation on slum conditions and a fetish for unusual names.

398
... that Mark Twain is one of the few great American authors that children will actually bother to read.

399
... that Gertrude Stein was redundant, which is to say repetitious, and therefore she ran on and on and on and on and on and on in such a way as to use more words than necessary in making her point, and in so doing...

400
... that if an author has a best seller with one book, the next will do almost as well, regardless of how good it is.

Language & Literature — Analysis

We live in an era of overspeak. There are simply too many communications directed at Americans: personal, commercial, political. There is a great revulsion at the thought of wasted words (381-382, 388, 394-395). Literature is seen as a pseudosophistication of the upper class or of rebellious academics who have rejected the Middle Class Credo. Therefore, the view of literature, and professors of literature, is not favorable (393-394, 397-399).

MARRIAGE & FAMILY

401

... that men raise their social class by education and financial success while women raise their social class by marrying a man of a higher social class.

402

... that when a man marries a woman of a higher social class, his class does not go up, hers goes down.

403

... that a middle class wife who behaves in a lower class fashion will be thoroughly criticized by her husband's relatives and associates.

404

... that people try to get married in order to prove that they are worth loving.

405

... that when people are ready to get married, they will do so with the first person of the opposite sex who meets certain minimum standards and is interested in the venture.

406

... that after men get married, they gain weight; and if a man does not gain weight after getting married, his wife is not a good cook.

407

... that men and women do things in front of their spouse that they did not do in front of their fiance.

408

... that when checking into a motel, newlyweds try to conceal the fact that they are on their honeymoon, but an older couple on their second honeymoon will brag about the fact.

409
... that there are no perfect marriages but some are better than others.

410
... that some marriages are not worth saving.

411
... that most divorces occur because neither person has tried hard e-nough.

412
... that no one from California ever won Paul Harvey's tournament of roses.

413
... that it is rare for a middle class woman to walk out on her husband; she would prefer to go to court and win the house and support payments.

414
... that women who drive large station wagons put their family first.

415
... that the wife of an alcoholic deserves pity.

416
... that the woman who divorces a physically disabled man is reprehens-ible.

417
... that if anyone makes your spouse's life miserable, your life will be-come miserable.

418
... that most men go to lodges or on hunting/fishing trips to get away from their wives.

419
... that most men would prefer to be polygamists, if it were legal, socially acceptable and if they could afford it.

. . . that celebrity status makes a successful marriage less likely.

. . . that no matter how many toothbrushes there are in the bathroom, people can always tell which is theirs.

. . . that in-laws turn out to be a blessing or a curse.

. . . that the worst thing about holidays is being unable to avoid social gatherings with relatives you despise.

. . . that in every large family gathering, there is always one sourpuss that everyone else wishes were not there.

. . . that people without family feel very depressed over the holidays.

. . . that most old bachelors are bashful.

. . . that most young bachelors are too wild to settle down.

Marriage & Family — Analysis

Marriage and family form the backbone of stable, civilized society (at least, that is what the middle class believes). Getting married is a sort of irrational compulsion sought for unconscious psycho-social motives (401-405, 425). Marriage is full of minor frustrations (407, 415, 417, 423-424) and possibilities for heartaches. Marriage is definitely not *the* source of personal fulfillment (418-419), especially for men.

Perhaps the future will be brighter, with less remnants of patriarchal culture (401-402) and unresolved mental conflicts (404-405) determining the decision to marry. If each team can be the result of a better selection process, and the rules can be formulated to the mutual satisfaction of both members of the team, the resulting game should be a lot more fun.

MEN & WOMEN

428
... that women are more concerned about social class than men are.

429
... that girls from lower class families have their first child at age 17, while middle class women have their first child after finishing college and starting a career, usually in their 30's.

430
... that when lower class women begin to age, they do not attempt to reverse the process with exercise.

431
... that lower class women are only attracted to macho men, while middle class women are attracted to men who offer economic security.

432
... that when a lower class man does not succeed with a woman, he attributes this to be insufficiently macho, but when a middle class man does not succeed with a woman, he attributes it to being insufficiently sensitive.

433
... that a middle class male is uncomfortable in a room full of lower class males; a lower class female is uncomfortable in a room full of middle class females.

434
... that men of all races prefer lighter skinned women.

435
... that motorists are more likely to stop and give a ride to a female hitchhiker than a male one; and this is either because the motorist wishes to take advantage of her or wishes to warn her of other motorists.

... that you rarely get a chance to meet the people that you see in public to whom you are most attracted.

... that in a romantic relationship, the person who is less emotionally involved will manipulate the person who is more emotionally involved; if neither side is emotionally involved, the relationship will break up at the first attempt to manipulate; if both parties are emotionally involved to a great degree, this results in marriage (or at least a long term relationship with mutual manipulation).

... that few men will offer a seat to a woman on a crowded bus anymore, unless she is attractive or wearing a low cut dress.

... that most men feel better about looking at themselves in the mirror than most women do.

... that in a bus station one sees some very beautiful women and some very homely women; in an airport, one sees some very beautiful women and some very homely women; but the homely women in the airport do a better job of covering up the fact.

... that if a man first sees a woman at a distance, his first impression of her is determined by hair, figure and clothes; if a man first meets a woman at close range, his first impression of her is determined by her face; if a man first meets a woman over the telephone, his first impression of her is drastically altered when he sees her in person.

... that many photogenic people are not beautiful; many beautiful people are not photogenic, but most are.

... that men have stronger underarm odor than women.

... that when a man is desperate, any woman looks good enough; when a man is sexually stimulated, he may promise just about anything.

445
... that rich widows, no matter how homely, attract more attention from men than do poor widows with an apartment full of kids.

446
... that old maids are sorry they didn't when they could've.

447
... that a middle class woman feels uneasy walking down a city street with a cigarette in her mouth.

448
... that women athletes are more masculine than non-athletes; the most successful women athletes have hormonal abnormalities.

449
... that fashion models have a facial expression that indicates contempt or physical discomfort.

450
... that the women in comic books were drawn by the same artists who designed the tops of pinball machines.

451
... that women on welfare are physically repulsive.

452
... that at country clubs and yacht harbors, the wives are invariably younger and more attractive than their husbands.

453
... that women who walk with a wide stride are more assertive.

454
... that before women became assertive, they fainted.

455
... that any man opposed to the E.R.A. will be branded as a sexist or chauvinist pig by its supporters.

... that women activists use little or no deodorant.

... that housewives who do not have enough to do gossip on the phone and watch soap operas.

... that women are more afraid of crawling things than men are.

... that women are more grouchy when pregnant, going through menopause, or just before menstruation.

... that women with less than a 38D wish they had a bigger bust; men under 6'2" wish they were taller.

... that beautiful women should not be upset with men who gawk, unless they are obnoxious about it; women who dress seductively have no right at all to be upset with men who gawk.

... that in the early 1970's, a majority of women were not wearing bras, and at that time men got into the habit of looking carefully to determine whether or not a woman was wearing a bra; although by the late 1970's most women were again wearing bras in public, men have not been able to break this habit; many women are aware of this and wear bras which make them look braless in order to get more masculine attention.

... that lower class people feel guilty if they do not raise boys to be he-men and girls to be sexpots, but middle class people feel guilty if they treat their sons and daughters differently in any way.

... that middle class people are more embarrassed if their daughters look like sexpots than if they look like slobs.

... that heavy perfume will turn off family, friends and acquaintances, but strange men will follow a woman for several blocks if her perfume trail is strong enough.

466

. . . that if a girl is loose enough with her affections, she can get the attention of men, no matter how homely she is; if a girl is beautiful enough, she can get the attention of men no matter how cold she is.

Men & Women — Analysis

Greater class consciousness (428) in females was noted by Packard (1959) and can be attributed to the fact that female social class was more determined by marital rather than career status (401-402). Middle class women have a certain idealized image of how they should be: beautiful, intelligent, controlling their own lives and manipulating their men, securing deference of all those beneath them in social class and being accepted as an equal by everyone else. In order to accomplish all of these objectives, the middle class woman must have all the seductive powers of a courtesan, but not be viewed as a slut.

Lower class women are seen as those who have fallen short of these ideals. They are ugly hags (430, 439-440, 451-452), manipulated by brutal men (431-432), and lose control of their lives by getting pregnant as teenagers (429). Lower class women strive to gain what middle class women strive for, but lack the middle class sense of restraint and patience. The lower class woman who tries to better herself does so by trying to look like the woman on the tops of pinball machines (450, remember it is the lower class men who play pinball). Middle class women criticize these lower class strivers for looking like sexpots (457, 463-466). This is one reason why lower class women are uncomfortable in the presence of middle class women (433); the one thing they can do to advance themselves works only with males.

It is difficult to predict what changes the future will bring. Lower class parents raise their sons differently from their daughters (Kohn, 1969) and thereby perpetuate these differences in the next generation. Middle class parents, on the other hand, seem to be moving in the direction of a unisexual standard of childrearing: the goal is no longer to have one's daughter marry a physician, but to have her become a physician.

Career women may represent a version of the middle class ideal but they pose a threat to the self-esteem of two segments of the middle class: career men who are insecure about their competence and prospects for advancement, and women who feel ashamed that they are only home-makers. Perhaps the career woman will become the norm for the next generation of middle class women, and could relieve middle class men of the double bind their nagging wives now place them in: "We need more money, you've got to get that promotion. . . .You don't spend enough time with me!" Working wives increase their family income and reduce their emotional dependency on their husbands.

MINOR FRUSTRATIONS

467

... that everyone has wet his pants at least once in public, and most people get the idea that they should try to pretend that water has been splashed on them; as a result, anyone who has water splashed on them will be suspected of having urinated.

468

... that the only thing more boring than researching one's own genealogy is listening to someone else recite theirs.

469

... that street numbers are very difficult to read when one is driving down an unknown street.

470

... that umbrellas are frustrating to open, close, carry along, walk with and dry off, but most frustrating when forgotten.

471

.. that most of the time elevators take so long that it would have been quicker to use stairs; the exceptional elevators which are fast bother the internal organs.

472

... that just when you have to start thinking about saving for your retirement, you have to start worrying about putting your kids through college and helping out aged relatives.

473

... that the temperature signs on two banks within a block of each other do not agree.

... that when men live alone, they do not bother to lift the toilet seat and foreign men never bother.

475
... that government offices are never open when most working people have the time to go there.

476
... that streets in need of repaving do not get it; streets which are repaved are those streets which you have to use or those on which you park your car.

477
... that it is extremely difficult to water indoor hanging plants without spilling any water.

478
... that a snowfall is pretty, but not in the city.

479
... that every other weekend, some church, school or service group is holding a bazaar, pancake breakfast or barbecue.

480
... that there is nothing messier than a broken egg that does not go where it is supposed to go.

481
... that most people spend more money for the postage on mail order contests than they make in winnings.

482
... that telephone booths do not do a very good job of keeping out street noises.

483
... that when a wrong price is rung up at the checkstand of a super-market, it is a higher price.

484
... that the greatest stimulus for infant urination is the feel of a clean

diaper.

485
... that Christmas decorations are put up too early by most businesses, and small cities are even worse.

486
... that when you have asked someone for directions, and they do not know but are trying to tell you something, it is very hard to break off conversation with them and get on your way.

487
... that before the days of high-powered audio equipment, the biggest noise in the suburbs was from power mowers and barking dogs; the biggest noise in apartments was from family arguments.

488
... that the signs which advertise garage sales refer to some previous weekend.

489
... that the metric system is much easier to use, provided you do not have to convert anything to or from the old system.

490
... that too many cities and streets have the same or very similar names.

491
... that before the invention of the photocopy machine, there was a lot less paperwork.

492
... that no one enjoys filling out the thank you cards for bridal, shower or anniversary gifts.

493
... that anyone who answers a phone call after five rings must have been sitting on the toilet.

494
... that half the time the telephone answering machine responds, the person in the house does not want to answer the phone until the caller can be

identified.

495

... that the people who hang up before leaving a message on the telephone answering machine were not worth calling back anyway, but the people who left a message on the answering machine when the tape jammed had something important to say and will not be calling back.

496

... that service stations clean their restrooms after each 10,000 customers.

497

... that half of the time, restrooms in bus stations and airports are closed for cleaning, the other half of the time, these restrooms are in need of cleaning.

498

... that the shelves and ledges in public restrooms are neither large nor strong enough to support binders, briefcases or shopping bags.

Minor Frustrations — Analysis

Whole books have been written about minor frustrations, cataloging them as corollaries to Murphy's Law (Dickson, 1980). Most of these credos depict something which middle class people find frustrating because it interferes with the middle class objectives of convenience and efficiency. Other themes are things which lead to waste (481, 483, 496-497) or embarrassment (467).

MOVIES

499

... that movies were better in the 1930's.

500

... that remakes of classic movies are never as good as the originals, but make more money.

501

... that in modern movies, visual effects have replaced acting.

502

... that Orson Welles was a genius.

503

... that "The Sound of Music" is a wholesome movie.

504

... that it is safe to take the kids and grandma to anything made by Disney studios, but after age 10 (8 in California) kids develop a strange aversion to anything put out by Disney studios.

505

... that the viewers of X-rated movies do not care about the plot.

506

... that successful war, space and western movies must have good guys and bad guys.

507

... that Alfred Hitchcock gave a cameo appearance in everyone of his motion pictures.

... that no movie will ever be a failure at the box office if it has a beautiful woman and enough publicity.

... that people who demonstrate, protest, or speak out against a movie or book only make other people more interested in seeing it.

... that if their son or daughter gains a major part in a high school musical or play, lower class parents are elated, proud, bragging and already planning on having expensive cars when their child becomes a Hollywood star; but middle class parents respond by worrying that their child will attempt to pursue a theatrical career instead of going on to college or taking over the family business.

... that in the summer, drive-in movies last too late because of daylight saving time; the rest of the year, the weather is too bad to enjoy a drive-in, so only teenagers and people with large families frequent drive-in theatres and the people with large families are not able to enjoy the movie; only the teenagers are enjoying themselves at a drive-in, but not by watching the movie.

... that no one really understands what Marshall McLuhan meant when he said, "The medium is the message," but many dilettantes and pseudo-intellectuals repeat that phrase at opportune moments as if they understood what it meant.

Movies – Analysis

The majority of the American middle class has an attitude toward motion pictures that is a combination of nostalgia for or veneration of the past, and a disgust with present productions (499-501). Middle class people with family have a decided preference for "wholesome" films (503-504). Lower class people and adolescents go to the movies because it is a social event (511) or because they are fascinated with the sex, violence or visual effects. For older middle class people to go to today's movies, they must make it a social event by pretending that there is some sort of profound intellectual statement or aesthetic creation behind the boring and offensive things which come to pass on the screen (502).

Hollywood is a place where instant wealth and fame is given to men for extraordinary machismo and women for extraordinary seductiveness; at least this is what the lower class hopes for and the middle class fears most (510).

MUSIC

513

... that Bing Crosby was the greatest recording artist of the 1930's; Frank Sinatra was the greatest recording artist of the 1940's; Elvis Presley was the greatest recording artist of the 1950's; the Beatles were the greatest recording artists of the 1960's; the greatest recording artists of the 1970's were the sound studio technicians who mixed a dozen tracks to produce a disco record.

514

... that most people are extremely proud of the fact that they like a certain kind of music.

515

... that very few people in prison listen to Lawrence Welk.

516

... that the kind of music a person listens to is an indicator of personality; the volume at which someone listens to music is an indicator of consideration.

517

... that lower class people carry large battery-powered stereos while middle class people carry small battery-powered units with headphones, both out of an attempt to be elite.

518

... that the same country-western singer who convincingly portrays an alcoholic adulterer is sincere when he sings gospel.

519

... that lower class people have no appreciation of classical music.

... that people who go to a classical concert the first time clap between movements.

... that even people who are not opera fans talk about Luciano Pavarotti.

... that everybody enjoyed Arthur Fiedler and the Boston Pops.

... that deaths due to stampedes of crowds occur in third world nations or at rock concerts.

... that Punk Rock is a fad that has already peaked.

Music — Analysis

Nostalgia and disgust are also emotions which apply to contemporary music. In the past, musical tastes were determined by ethnic and regional differences rather than social class (with the possible exception of classical music, 519). Now, generational differences are most important. In each decade, the contemporary forms of music have been championed by the young. The baby boom generation made rock so popular in the 1960's by swelling the percentage of adolescents in the population. That generational cohort has now hit early middle age and creates a demand for "oldies" or "easy rock." Current trends in popular music are so uncreative (or at least are perceived as such) because today's adolescents constitute such a small percentage of the population.

Class differences can be seen more in how people play their music. Lower class people and adolescents identify with the lyrics and rhythm and imagine that other people who know that they are listening to the music will perceive them as being powerful, attractive and "cool" (or whatever the present slang term is). Therefore, adolescents and lower class people "publicize" their musical tastes with high volume (517-517) or bumper stickers, T-shirts, posters, fan magazines, etc.

NAMES

525
... that Anglo-Saxon names are out; Celtic names are in.

526
... that 60 years ago, every other child had a bliblical name or one beginning with the letter E; 30 years ago every other little girl was named Linda, Sue, Cathy or Barbara, and every other little boy was named John, David, Tom, Jim, or something ending in the letter Y.

527
... that today every other little girl is named Tanya, Ashley, Jennifer or Dawn, and every other little boy is named Eric, Scott, Bryan, Jason or Shaun.

528
... that since World War II, no child has been named Adolf; since Watergate, no child has been named Richard.

529
... that since Borden came out with Elsie the Cow and Elmer the Bull, no children have been given these names.

530
... that since the success of the TV program, "All In The Family," no child has been named Archie or Edith.

531
... that there are no more little girls being named Ethyl, Edna, Gladys, Phyllis, Wanda, Myrtle or Myra; while there are not more little boys being named Malcolm, Edgar or Cyrl.

532
... that a husband is flattered if his wife suggests naming their son after

him.

533

... that when naming their children, lower class people think of how the name would sound for an athlete or entertainer, but middle class people think of how the name would sound for a successful individual in business, medicine or politics.

534

... that before parents name their child, they think of other people they know who already have that name and reject it if they do not like any of those people.

535

... that no parents think of the resulting combination of initials before they name their child.

536

... that every other Black person has a name beginning with DE or LE.

537

... that twins should not be dressed alike or given similar sounding names.

538

... that people with first names that look like last names are more distinguished.

539

... that women who prefer to use the title Miss are more traditional, while those who insist on Ms are proud of the fact that they are not virgins (or embarrassed by the fact that they still are).

540

... that a woman who simply puts a Mrs. in front of her husband's name (e.g., refers to herself as Mrs. John Smith) believes that her husband is recognized as an important person.

541

... that if a woman keeps her maiden name (e.g., Jones) at work, her co-workers will probably address her husband as "Mr. Jones" the first time they meet him even though they know that Jones is the woman's maiden name.

... that a husband who hyphenates his own name to include his wife's maiden name will really try hard to make the marriage work.

... that there are no more dogs named Rover or Fido.

... that people cannot resist the temptation of giving poodles French names.

Names — Analysis

Names project various images, including status (533). We all respond to people and they respond to us and names are verbal forms that mediate this exchange. We do not want ourselves or our children to be regarded as "old-fashioned" (526), or associated with something bad (528, 534), or ridiculous (529-530). There are fashions and fads in names (525, 527, 531) and even cautious and conservative middle class people do not want to make their children conspicuous with an archaic or unusual name.

The attributions we make to the formal titles people put in front of their names (Dr., Mrs., etc., 539-540) and the way married women handle surnames (541-542) tell us something about how we view changing male-female roles. In the future, how shall we address Jane Smith after she marries George Johnson? One thing is certain: most middle class people will go along with whatever appears to be most acceptable to the group that they most identify with.

OLDER PEOPLE

545
... that lower class men feel old when the heavyweight boxing champion is younger; middle class men feel old when their boss is younger.

546
... that no matter how old, educated or successful you become, your parents will still give you unsolicited advice.

547
... that no one refers to himself as middle aged.

548
... that all this talk about male menopause has caused a lot of men to go through one.

549
... that beyond a certain age, people begin a second childhood, but no one will admit being that age at which the second childhood is entered.

550
... that young children and old women are never embarrassed by anything they say.

551
... that grandparents spoil the children.

552
... that most people cannot save enough for the dream vacation until they reach the age when they are too old to enjoy it.

553
... that if a door was left open, or the faucet let running, or a toilet unflushed, the guilty party is either under 10 or over 70.

... that most old people would feel a whole lot better if they just had someone to talk to.

... that old people purposely take a long time fumbling with change at cash registers in order to have an extra moment to talk with the clerk about their personal lives.

... that there are more old widows than old widowers.

... that old widowers have more fun than old widows.

... that old people reach a point where they add a year or two when reporting their ages.

... that old people get confused and start calling their grandchildren by their children's names.

... that old people never forget the details of their operations, nor tire of discussing them.

... that old people do not forget what happened 50 years ago but they do forget that they have already told you about it 50 times.

... that whenever you criticize an old person, and there is no other defense, the response will be, "Just wait until you get old."

... that the most difficult thing about living with an able-bodied, older relative is not waiting on them but trying to survive their attempts to be helpful.

There are, in contemporary American society, no clearcut guidelines about when someone is old (545, 547, 549) or how people are supposed to treat elders: as equals, as minors, as parents? There is the realization that old people like (and many desperately need) interpersonal contact (554-555).

Two factors have brought about the disruption of the multi-generational household. One is mobility, both geographical and social, so that the young generation moves away from the old. This is not only true in the United States but also in third world countries wherever people have left rural areas and headed for opportunities in urban areas. The second factor is that most American adults realize that old people can be a burden and bother in the home. What they say can be critical (546), outlandish (550), or boring (560-561). Their forgetfulness and rigid ways are problems when they do things (553, 563). They may interfere in domestic affairs (551). The worst thing of all is that it is very hard to correct them (552). For these reasons, it is unlikely that the multi-generational household will return in America unless economic imperatives dictate otherwise.

OPINIONS

564

... that everyone has an opinion on...

565

... that people become opinionated about wines after they have tasted more than three varieties.

566

... that people have opinions on many issues that they do not understand.

567

... that people without a college education lack the capacity to form their own opinions; they merely regurgitate what they have heard from others, while college educated people can come up with their own opinions because they have read the thoughts of the greatest thinkers in history.

568

... that the only one who cares about what the man-in-the-street said in his interview is the man who was in the street being interviewed.

569

... that you'll be sorry if you get into an argument with someone who drives a car with more than two bumper stickers.

570

... that the most argumentative people enjoy calling into radio talk shows.

People overestimate their own intelligence (566), taste (565), and persuasiveness and, therefore, overestimate the degree to which other people will be interested in hearing them present their opinions (568, 570).

PETS

571

... that lower class people rarely take their pets to spay and neuter clinics.

572

... that if you feed a stray animal, it will hang around your home hoping to be fed again.

573

... that some dogs in the United States live better than most people in underdeveloped countries.

574

... that a chasing dog will turn and cower if one stands one's ground.

575

... that dogs look for a fire hydrant or tree when urinating and for a nice green lawn when defecating.

576

... that lower class people let their dogs run free and then beat them brutally when they get into trouble, while middle class people either send their dogs to obedience school or keep them in the backyard.

577

... that everybody has heard the story about the poodle that exploded after being placed in the microwave oven to dry off.

578

... that people who own habitually barking dogs are not themselves bothered by the noise and are quite offended if you complain to them about it.

... that Americans feel an obligation to take their dogs for a ride.

... that people who likes dogs appreciate loyalty and spontaneity, while people who prefer cats appreciate independence.

... that dogs and cats do not enjoy traveling in the tiny cages provided for them by airlines and buses.

... that middle class girls go through a stage around age 12 in which they are infatuated with horses, and this subsides when they discover boys.

... that pet rocks are obedient and clean and cheaper to maintain than dogs, cats, fish or birds.

Pets — Analysis

Centuries ago most domesticated animals had economic utility as sources of food, beasts of burden, partners in the hunt or protection against hostile humans or undesirable animals. Now the role of animals in most urban and suburban areas is to serve as surrogate children. So, middle class pet owners take this role very seriously and try to treat their pets well (573, 579) and make them responsible creatures (or at least be responsible for them, 571, 576, 578).

PLACES

584
... that the country is the best place to raise children.

585
... that country folk take longer to warm up to you because they are genuine.

586
... that no town in America is named "Capital City" except in fiction.

587
... that cities which paint pictures on their fire hydrants are attempting to change their image.

588
... that cheap hotels in large cities cater mostly to winos and prostitutes.

589
... that New Yorkers are arrogant and pushy.

590
... that 40 years ago New York was a wonderful place to live; 20 years ago New York was a wonderful place to visit; if we could get rid of the crime in New York, it would be a wonderful place to visit; if we could get rid of the expense of caring for all the poor people, New York would be a wonderful place to live.

591
... that legalizing casino gambling could make any city a prosperous resort.

592
... that the Smithsonian Institution is the world's finest museum.

593

.. that if Washington, D.C. did not have the Smithsonian, government buildings or historical monuments, it would not be worth visiting.

594

... that old buildings which are not torn down become historical monuments.

595

... that Houston and Los Angeles are simply too big and congested.

596

... that Rochester is about as exciting as Philadelphia without the Liberty Bell.

597

... that in Chicago, spring occurs one afternoon in May or June, every other year.

598

... that Chicago's Sears Building may be taller than the Empire State Building, but it is not as impressive.

599

... that Pittsburgh and Oakland are not very nice places to live but they have good sports teams.

600

... that all children enjoy Disneyland and adults enjoy it more than they thought they would.

601

... that Californians can never understand why anyone prefers to live anywhere else.

602

... that each fall there are severe brush fires in southern California, and many thousands of acres of grassland and some expensive homes burn; each January there are record rains in southern California, and expensive homes are destroyed by mudslides.

603

... that the weather in Pasadena on New Years Day is picture perfect.

604

... that California has a disproportionately high number of bizarre murders.

605

... that only in northern California would people object to spraying to control dangerous insects.

606

... that anyone who has been to San Francisco is as proud of the fact as if he owned some of its prime real estate.

607

... that in California there is no stigma attached to being divorced.

608

... that the descendants of the Okies who moved to California in the dust bowl days are working as mechanics, carpenters or country western singers.

609

... that the people who came to California from Oklahoma were riffraff, while the people who came from the East were the cream of the crop, looking for new opportunities.

610

... that people in Utah are pretty nice, even the ones who are not Mormons.

611

... that the South is not as bad a place to live as it used to be.

612

... that the escape of chlorine gas due to a railroad tank-car derailment occurs every other month in a small southern town.

613

... that people from the Midwest never seem to catch on when they are boring you.

614

... that "All Star Bowling" is still a popular TV show in the Midwest.

615

... that little towns in the Midwest still have a 4th of July picnic with marching bands, hot dogs, sack races and baking contests.

616

... that there is less divorce in the Midwest, probably because people stay in boring marriages because they remember how boring it was to be single in the Midwest.

617

... that people from the northern states claim that they love the change of seasons.

618

... that Kansas is particularly boring to drive through.

619

... that most of the people who report sightings of UFO's live in little out-of-the-way places and could never get any notoriety any other way.

620

... that people from Ohio and New Jersey seem slightly embarrassed by the fact.

621

... that any vacation to Europe must include Paris in the itinerary, even though it is outrageously expensive and the people are incredibly rude.

622

... that lower class people can only dream about a vacation to Waikiki, San Juan or Acapulco, but so many middle class people have been going to these tropical resorts that even middle class people are beginning to consider them tacky, while upper class vacationers have considered these places tacky for 15 years.

623

... that any motel within 10 miles of a body of water has a name like "Shores," or "Surf," or "Beach."

... that some small motels have one-way mirrors over the bed.

Places — Analysis

Where one lives and where one vacations has many implications for status (601, 606, 619-620, 622). There are many stereotypical generalizations about places and their residents, just as there are about sexes, races, ages. These reflect the minor (and even major) frustrations of people who live or vacation there, as well as the deprecations of people who do not live there or go there and wish to feel that they are superior to it. So, most credos about places are negative until people have to defend why they live where they do. Most places are either portrayed as "big, bad cities" (588, 590, 595, 599), or boring (596, 613, 614, 616, 618). California has some areas which are neither, but they have too many "wacko" people running around (604) and many natural disasters (602), including the big earthquake that will make it fall into the sea. Two mid-westerners will complain about the weather (597) but when a Californian comes in, they become resolved not to lose status over a minor frustration and exclaim how they love the change of seasons (617) and would find California weather boring.

POLITICS

625
... that liberals do not admit the fact to the voters, preferring to call themselves moderates.

626
... that conservatives do not admit the fact to the voters, preferring to call themselves moderates.

627
... that conservatives are for less spending, less bureaucracy, less government regulations (except in the area of morality), and less leniency with the communists abroad and criminals at home.

628
... that liberals want to give more money to the poor at home and abroad.

629
... that Democrats want whatever bureaucrats, labor leaders, welfare loafers and pointy-headed intellectuals want.

630
... that Republicans want what big business wants.

631
... that the Libertarians have a lot of good ideas which would probably not work.

632
... that if middle class people are Democrats, they try to justify this by expressing concern for those persons less fortunate than they.

633

... that the typical delegate to the Democratic National Convention is a public school teacher that belongs to a union.

634

... that the typical delegate to the Republican National Convention is the proprietor of a small business or the wife of a professional or executive.

635

... that when the political convention is over, the losers get on the stand with the winners and express unity.

636

... that Harry Truman used more profanity than any other president.

637

... that Harry Truman was a great president but no one knew that when he was in office.

638

... that every succeeding president has hoped that history would be as kind to him as it was to Harry Truman.

639

... that Calvin Coolidge was the most quiet politician in American history.

640

... that Franklin Delano Roosevelt brought about more change than any other president.

641

... that Tip O'Neill is a caricature of a politician and a sore loser.

642

... that Hitler was insane but Mussolini was just foolish.

643

... that Abraham Lincoln was honest, homely, courageous and witty.

644

... that Herbert Hoover was a great man but should not have been president in 1929.

645

... that Winston Churchill was a great leader.

646

... that MacArthur would have been a strong president.

647

... that Anwar Sadat was the greatest head of state during this half of the century.

648

... that if Will Rogers had gone into government, he would have put some common sense into things.

649

... that a lot of people lost respect for Eisenhower a few years after he left office but Eisenhower has gained a great deal of respect in the past few years.

650

... that a hundred years from now people will still be debating about whether or not John Kennedy's assassination was a conspiracy.

651

... that Lyndon Johnson looked like a better president in 1964 than in 1968.

652

... that the press had it in for Nixon and Agnew.

653

... that the people who had been voting against Nixon since the 1950's were delighted when Watergate broke.

654

... that Gerald Ford's most significant act as president was pardoning his predecessor.

... that the most memorable aspect of the Ford administration was his wife's outspokenness.

... that at least Ford was more honest than Nixon.

... that Carter was just as honest as Ford and even more intelligent, but did not accomplish anything either.

... that when Carter ran for the presidency in 1976, he was vague on the issues and when he ran for re-election in 1980, the voters still did not know where he stood on the issues.

... that we did not prove very much by not going to the Olympics in 1980 but it was one of the few difficult decisions that Carter actually made.

... that Reagan is not as smart or hardworking as Carter but he has some courage and has accomplished a lot.

... that Reagan does not care about the disadvantaged.

... that Jerry Brown is an opportunist who waffles on the issues.

... that whatever the politicians promise you today, you will be paying for tomorrow, whether or not you get it.

... that it is hard to believe that there is an energy crisis when the president flies Air Force One a thousand miles for a "working weekend" several times a month.

... that every conference of mayors or state governors results in a call for more federal aid and less federal controls.

666
... that people who believe it is their duty to vote will vote for every office, even when they do not know who is running; and on every proposition, even the ones that they do not understand.

667
... that political campaigns take too much time and money.

668
... that most voters have very short memories; that is why they return incumbents to office.

669
... that it is difficult to go into politics and remain honest.

670
... that the primary concern of all presidents is to win re-election, and when that is accomplished, they worry about how they will go down in history.

671
... that the Supreme Court has overstepped its bounds on the issue of...

672
... that a few off-the-record comments to the wrong journalist can end any political career.

673
... that politicians think that they can fool enough people long enough to get elected.

674
... that only a rich man can afford to run for office.

675
... that public financing of elections is a wasteful subsidy to the politicians.

676
... that retired politicians and military never have a problem finding jobs

as consultants.

677

... that many contributions to political candidates are made on the basis of chances of winning rather than similarity of political philosophy.

678

... that inherited wealth is a prime factor in promoting inequality.

679

... that inheritance taxes which widows and orphans have to pay are the most cruel taxes.

680

... dictatorships attempt simple solutions to complex problems; democracies attempt complex solutions to simple problems.

681

... that the government should do something about...

682

... that when the government tries to do something about..., it either passes an unenforceable law or creates an ineffectual bureaucracy.

Politics — Analysis

The middle class is thoroughly alienated from American politics, which seems to benefit the rich by giving power and prestige to upper class officeholders (674) and those who finance them (630, 677), while giving entitlement services and cash benefits to the lower class (628-629). The middle class is given the privilege of paying for government. To a great extent, the blame for this state of affairs falls on the middle class voters who do not have sufficient understanding (666) of the fact that it is impossible to meet their contradictory goals. Middle class people want what both liberals and conservatives promise (627-628), but are dissatisfied with what the Democrats and Republicans end up doing to them (629-630, 663). The politicians are aware of this confusion of issues and do their utmost to use it to their own advantage (625-626, 658, 662, 673).

PRESS

683
... that middle class people feel guilty if they do not make an effort to read the newspaper or hear the news.

684
... that people are very proud of subscribing to the *New York Times* or *Wall Street Journal*.

685
... that reporters would rather write stories to increase circulation than tell the truth.

686
... that when nothing really important is happening, the press will do anything to make something look like a scandal.

687
... that one problem with the news is that it gets people all flustered over so many things that they can do nothing about.

688
... that the cartoons in the *New Yorker* are not funny.

689
... that Sunday papers are too heavy.

690
... that if the newspaper made an error and printed the wrong astrological signs with the predictions, no one would be able to tell the difference.

691
... that more people read the astrology column than admit to believing

in it.

... that the photographs in the tabloids look retouched.

... that most of the stories in the *National Enquirer* are either false or else gross exaggerations but, nevertheless, there are many good things in there that cannot be found elsewhere.

Press — Analysis

The middle class' low opinion of the press is partly due to a reaction to the excess communication in our society (689) and partly due to the fact that people in the press have at least two similarities to the people in politics: they contribute to the surplus of information (686, 693) and seek to profit by it (685). What keeps both politicians and journalists in their jobs is that middle class people feel that it is their duty to read newspapers (683) and vote.

Of course, the solution is neither to stop reading nor to stop voting but to develop enough insight, analytical skill and clarity of purpose so we can convert information into wisdom and then convert wisdom into effective personal and social action.

PRODUCTS

694

... that never before have Americans had so many gadgets.

695

... that most presents are things that you don't need, wouldn't use or already have.

696

... that when more than two neighbors or friends acquire a new gadget, it ceases to be a luxury.

697

... that fireplaces may be less efficient than woodburning stoves but they are more fun to watch.

698

... the environmentalists will not be happy until we have to wash our clothes by hand and hang them up to dry in our sweltering apartments.

699

... that when people consider the cost of their snapshots, they consider the cost of the film, not the cost of the flashbulbs, camera, batteries or processing.

700

... that you can learn a lot about people from an examination of their garbage.

701

... that few kids are playing pinball now that there are video games.

702

... that the ballpoint pen is one of the cleanest and most convenient ways of writing ever invented, but it is one of the most boring ways of writing ever invented.

703

... that things sold by mail order are not good enough to be sold in stores.

704

... that each year many useful inventions are stifled by corporations who have an economic interest in the thing that the new invention would replace.

705

... that the furniture used in model homes is smaller than normal furniture in order to give the rooms the illusion of being large.

706

... that Christmas is not Christmas without a Christmas tree.

707

... that dandruff shampoos do not work very well, and the ones that work the best smell like sheep dip.

708

... that they don't make ... like they used to.

709

... that people get more wrong numbers with a rotary dial than with a touch tone.

710

... that the people looking for the housebrands in the supermarket are middle class.

711

... that by 1985 people will see an old Rubik's cube and wonder why they spent so much time with it.

712

... that in 10 years, a culturally deprived home will be one without a computer.

713

... that it would be wonderful if headlights would turn off automatically as soon as the key is withdrawn from the ignition.

714

... that toilet paper does not work very well.

715

... that nobody sleeps well the first night on a waterbed.

716

... that Japanese products are of higher quality and lower price than their American counterparts.

717

... that middle class people feel unprepared if they do not have a years supply of batteries, fuses and lightbulbs on hand.

718

... that if two brands of a product have different prices, the higher priced brand is probably superior in quality.

719

... that the price of ... is outrageous.

720

... that the longer you wait to buy something, the more the price will rise.

721

... that you can really save some money if you wait for a sale.

722

... that supermarkets only have sales when they cannot get rid of something at the normal price or else want to get customers to go in and buy other, higher-priced merchandise.

723

... that if you save something long enough, it will either come back into style or become a collector's item.

Products — Analysis

Middle class Americans have come into possession of a great quantity of products (694) but the level of satisfaction with them is low. Many products just don't work that well (703, 707-708, 714, 716). Many products are too expensive (719) or wasteful (697). The system is maintained by deceptive practices in merchandising (705), suppression of better, more cost-effective products (704), and the middle class distorted ideas about status (696) or gift giving (695).

RACIAL MINORITIES

724
... that Japanese-Americans have the neatest front yards.

725
... that there are no Japanese-Americans on welfare or in jail in the state of California.

726
... that more white women go around with Black men than Black women go around with white men.

727
... that if a prostitute is with a well-dressed Black man, he is her pimp; but if a prostitute is with a well-dressed white man, he is her customer.

728
... that a child of mixed white/black ancestry is Black.

729
... that people who observe a mulatto child with a Black woman are impressed with how beautiful the child looks; people who observe a mulatto child with a white woman have doubts about the woman's morals.

730
... that Black people call each other "nigger" as a symbol of affection, but they regard the use of that word by white folks as an unforgiveable insult.

731
... that when in the company of a Black person, it is best for white persons not to bring up the subject of race unless the Black person brings it up first.

... that if a Black woman is anywhere close to being qualified for a job, she will get it over a white male who is well qualified.

... that when Blacks behave according to middle class norms, they are just as good as white people and even better than those white people who behave according to lower class norms.

... that anyone who opposes forced busing will be accused of being a racist by the supporters of forced busing.

... that the ethnic backgrounds that people brag about today are the same ethnic backgrounds that people were ashamed of 30 years ago.

... that since Pope John Paul II, there have been fewer Polish jokes.

... that Americans would not have any qualms about voting for a qualified candidate who happened to be Catholic, Black or female, but a Jewish candidate would have to demonstrate more loyalty to the United States than Israel in order to get the votes of Gentiles.

... that every other psychiatrist is a Jew who cannot stand the sight of blood but went to medical school because of parental pressure.

... that when Indians move off the reservation and into large cities, they get drunk and attempt to stay that way.

... that Puerto Ricans went to New York because it had the highest welfare benefits.

Sociologists have long maintained that the differences between white and Black Americans were reducible to differences in social class (Bloom, Whiteman & Deutsch, 1967). Middle class Americans have largely accepted social class as the basis for their prejudices. They generally do not have a great deal of prejudice toward racial minorities who accept the Middle Class Credo (724-725, 733), and sincerely desire to get along with all ethnic groups (731). However, the government's emphasis on the attainment of racial equality through affirmative action (732) and forced busing (734) has greatly alienated the white middle class.

Racial prejudice in lower class white Americans is stronger than that of middle class Americans. This is due to the fact that the lower class whites are at the bottom of white society and need to boost self-esteem by feeling superior to someone else, and since they cannot do this on the basis of occupation, income or education, they turn to race. It was also true in the past that lower class whites were more directly in competition with lower class Blacks for menial jobs.

These credos also reflect the resurgence of ethnic pride in the white middle class (525, 735) and the role of sexual myths, fears and fantasies in racial prejudice.

RECREATION & SPORTS

741
... that never before have Americans spent so much time or money on leisure activities.

742
... that more people are engaging in vigorous exercise today than 20 years ago.

743
... that baseball games are too slow.

744
... that baseball players are superstitious.

745
... that the goal of every big league baseball player is to earn enough money to purchase a beer distributorship or restaurant.

746
... that no statement by a baseball player recorded for broadcast is free of grammatical errors.

747
... that it was easier for baseball fans to get through the fifth week of the strike than the first week.

748
... that the kids in Little League go out of their way to make diving, one-handed catches.

749
... that the fans do not enjoy a no-hitter and do not even know that one is taking place until it is all over.

... that there are few Black quarterbacks and place-kickers in football, but few non-Blacks in pro basketball.

751

... that football and hockey have gotten too violent.

752

... that Pele is the world's favorite athlete.

753

... that Jim Thorpe was the best all-around athlete in history.

754

... that most boxers are not very intelligent but Sugar Ray Leonard is an exception to that.

755

... that boxers do not really believe all the things that they say about their opponents before a big match but have to make those outlandish statements in order to get more publicity.

756

... that after boxers retire, they put on weight.

757

.. that retired prize fighters talk about making a comeback.

758

... that boxers come from the lower class.

759

... that college and Olympic wrestling is a real sport but boring to watch; professional wrestling is a put-on but pretty interesting, at least for lower class audiences.

760

... that polo and sailing are upper class sports; the middle class has now moved into water skiing, snow skiing, tennis, racketball and golf.

761

... that Bjorn Borg is more of a gentleman than most other tennis players.

... that Howard Cosell is least popular among lower class sports fans.

... that people who like to backpack have middle class upbringing and are trying to rebel against it.

... that in order to unwind after a hard day's work, lower class men drink, smoke, work on junk cars, go to stock car races or engage in domestic violence; while middle class men jog, play tennis, tinker with a home computer or take some courses toward the completion of a graduate degree.

... that other board games are just takeoffs on monopoly or chess.

... that checker players have more common sense than chess players.

... that male card players are trying to show how clever and self-controlled they are, but female card players just enjoy the social contact.

... that the people who spend hours at coin-operated games are either minors or lower class.

... that no amount of practice could turn an uncoordinated person into an Olympic champion.

... that if America's professional athletes could compete in the Olympics, America would win more medals than all other nations combined; the idea of banning professional athletes is a communist plot to make their athletes look good competing against our amateurs.

This has become a major part of American life this century (741). The middle class seems to go in for recreations that involve mental stimulation or the maintenance of physical fitness (760, 764), but the lower class does not appreciate these motives (762) and is attracted by something which stimulates the senses (768), especially if it involves violence (759, 764). Professional sports are getting more violent (751), boring (743, 747) or ridiculous (755, 759).

RELIGION

771
... that religious leaders have always been talking about a resurgence of religion in America.

772
... that most of the radio and TV preachers have gotten pretty wealthy.

773
... that if there are two young men on bicycles and they have white shirts and are wearing ties, and their hair is short and neat, and they have fair skin, it is safe to assume that they are Mormon missionaries.

774
... that no reasonable person could believe the doctrines of the Mormon church but it just may be that having a happy family life is worth trying anything.

775
... that the Catholic church has opposed the most effective means of birth control because it wants more Catholics in the world.

776
... that in Catholic schools, the courses on marriage and sexuality are taught by priests or nuns.

777
... that Jehovah's Witnesses attract lower class people.

778
... that when skid row drunks get desperate, they fake religious conversions in order to get a warm meal or a place to sleep.

... that people standing on city streetcorners at 6:00 AM, who are not skid row bums or waiting for a bus, are missionaries.

780

... that people who join religious cults were mixed up before they joined; the only difference is that after they joined, they no longer believe they are mixed up.

781

.. that religious cults use brainwashing techniques.

782

... that people are not as afraid of going to hell as they used to be.

Religion – Analysis

Theologian Paul Tillich (1957) defined religion as a person's *ultimate concern*. Regardless of this definition, the majority of contemporary middle class Americans are not that concerned about religion. Only 1.1% of the credos in this book are devoted to religion. There is some cynicism about preachers being profiteers (772) and church doctrines being opposed to progress (775). The middle class considers religion to be the refuge of the lower class seeking solace (777), or the skid row bums (778) or mentally unbalanced (780) seeking to put their lives together. Perhaps the only middle class justification of religion is that it promotes some middle class virtues; such as, self-control, honesty, and family (774).

RESIDENCES

783
... that upper class people prefer to live on higher ground.

784
... that many slums were once rich suburbs.

785
... that middle class people feel deprived if they do not own their own residence and guilty if they have kids before purchasing a home with a big yard.

786
... that in middle class neighborhoods, there is less garbage in the street.

787
... that middle class people feel ashamed if their front yard has weeds, unraked leaves, unmowed lawn, or a junk car.

788
... that speculation in real estate has put the average single family dwelling beyond the means of the average American family.

789
... that men want to move to a larger house so they can have a gameroom, study or workshop; women want to move to a larger home so they will have more room for knick knacks.

790
... that people who own their own homes take better care of them than people who merely rent.

791
... that a man who has a nice backyard with a high fence does not have

to make so many trips to the bathroom.

792
... that people who live in houses can never understand how anyone can bear to be cooped up in a tiny apartment; people in apartments cannot understand how anyone can put up with all that yardwork.

793
... that for most people, trying to "do it yourself" takes so much time and involves so many problems that it is better to hire someone who knows what he is doing to do home repairs.

Residences — Analysis

Living at a certain address, even more so than living in a certain part of the country, has status implications. The middle class drive for acquiring the proper residence is not merely a quest for status. Also involved are the middle class virtues of cleanliness (786), responsibility to one's children (785), physical space for personal fulfillment (789) and privacy (791).

This middle class drive is greatly jeopardized by the speculation in real estate. Not only does this make it difficult for middle class people to purchase a home (788), it means that other houses in their neighborhood will be purchased by speculators and occupied by renters who may be of a lower social class and will probably be less concerned about the upkeep of the neighborhood (790).

SALESMEN

794

... that no matter what question you ask, and no matter what the truth is, a salesman will say what he thinks is necessary to get you to buy the product.

795

... that car salesmen never say, "Wait until next month, you'll get a better deal."

796

... that the door-to-door magazine salesmen who say they are involved in a scholarship contest are not.

797

... that salesmen are bullshitters in all areas of life and have a very high divorce rate.

Salesmen — Analysis

The middle class person's stereotypical views of sales personnel is unqualifiedly negative. This may be due to the fact that they are viewed as agents of deception (794, 796). However, if you ask people what *their* life insurance agent or car dealer is like, their opinion of that individual is quite positive. Either the stereotype has no validity and exists only to explain consumer's frustrations with products, or else salespersons are such good bullshitters that they charm consumers even though the consumers know what salespersons are really like.

SCIENCE & TECHNOLOGY

798

... that there has been more change in the past 20 years than in all previous human history.

799

... that science and technology can be used for good or evil.

800

... that whereas scientists used to wear white coats and write large equations on blackboards, now they work in their shirtsleeves at a computer terminal.

801

... that no one studies Morse code anymore.

802

... that before the year 2000, a new, cheap, abundant, non-polluting and safe source of energy will be found, but if the coal and oil companies have large reserves at this time, those companies will suppress the use of this new power source.

803

... that if all the money and brainpower that was spent on going to the moon had been spent on medical research, we would have had a cure for cancer.

Science & Technology — Analysis

Why only six credos about such a basic part of contemporary society? There are two explanations. One is that there are many credos which could have been placed in this section but have been placed elsewhere (e.g., 712).

Another perspective is that the belief that technological change is coming faster and faster is a myth. In the first quarter of the century, inventions (the automobile, radio, motion pictures) greatly impacted everyday life. The next quarter century saw widespread air travel and television. What technology has significantly modified everyday life in the past 30 years? The computer has affected the office and recordkeeping, but has not yet affected communication, transportation or homelife to a great degree. Certainly nothing as revolutionary as radio or the automobile has come about since 1950.

A great deal of the middle class attitude on technology is a sense of fear that it can be used for evil (798), or the frustration that neither corporate giants (802) nor politicians (803) will use technology to meet human needs.

SEX

804

... that once a girl has gone all the way, she will find it most difficult to stop at half the way in the future.

805

... that 20 years ago there were more frigid women, but less impotent men.

806

... that lower class men believe that they have more sexual potency than middle class men; middle class men believe that they have more control over their sexual instincts than lower class men do.

807

... that women are better able to tolerate sexual abstinence than men are.

808

... that many prissy schoolmarms and librarians go on vacations at swinging resorts, hundreds of miles away from their small communities, and have a real orgy for two weeks; those who don't go to such a resort at least fantasize about it.

809

... that men fear that their penis is smaller than average.

810

... that the penis of the Black male is larger than that of the white male.

811

... that by the time they are 15, boys in America have heard this story, told in earnest: "There was once a couple in the drive-in and the girl got scared and tightened and the guy could not get out and they had to call a doctor to get them apart."

812

... that alcohol makes women more pliant sexually but it diminishes performance in males.

813

... that if a husband has been out of town for more than a week and is not eager to have intercourse with his wife when he returns, he has been unfaithful.

814

... that husbands never worry about whether or not the kids will hear.

815

... that when a wife says that she does not want to have sex because she has a headache, she is saying that she has a headache because she does not want to have sex.

816

... that promiscuous people are trying to prove that they are attractive.

817

... that only abnormal children and abnormal old people think about sex, but only abnormal adult males fail to think about sex.

818

... that Latin and Middle Eastern men look for vaginal bleeding from their wives on the wedding night, and if these men see no blood, they suspect their wives were not virgins and beat them mercilessly, but do not denounce them in public for fear of retaliation from the wife's family.

819

... that people get extremely embarrassed when they are in the sex section of the library and are spotted by someone who knows them.

820

... that the achievement of simultaneous orgasm is proof of sexual compatibility.

821

... that farm boys have their first sexual experience in a hayloft.

822

... that high school and military hygiene films are a decade behind the times and produce more laughter than edification.

823

... that a man and a woman who check into a hotel without luggage are not married to each other and will not be staying the entire night.

824

... that sweetbreads are an aphrodisiac for males.

825

... that a Spanish Fly is a powerful aphrodisiac, but very dangerous.

826

... that birth control pills may cause cancer or heart disease but are less dangerous than pregnancy.

827

.. that lower class men are resistant to the use of condoms; lower class women frequently ignore birth control precautions, and that is why there are so many lower class people.

828

.. that virginity in boys is a disease and, unless cured, can lead to other diseases (e.g., homosexuality).

829

... that homosexuality and masturbation are less sinful than they used to be.

830

... that homosexuals are not so bad if they stay in the closet.

831

... that in homosexual couples, one has the role of the man and one has the role of the woman. .

832

... that lesbians hate men but they secretly long for a super-masculine male who will awaken their hidden feminity.

833

... that male homosexuals have a tendency to develop careers in cosmetology, fashion design or the performing arts.

834

... that homosexuals are not happy, even if they do insist on calling themselves gay.

835

... that sexual offenders tend to be repeaters.

836

... that obscene phone callers love it when the person stays on the line with them and gets upset.

837

... that wider availability of prostitution would reduce the frequency of sex crimes.

838

... that wider availability of pornography would increase the frequency of sex crimes.

839

... that B-girls are not really thirsty or interested in talking to the customers, but want their commission.

Sex — Analysis

Not only have contemporary Americans overestimated the technological revolution, they have overestimated the sexual revolution. It is more correct, in both cases, to speak of evolution rather than revolution, but some decades did show more change in behavior than others. The 1920's suggested that nice girls might (through motion pictures) and provided a place where they might (the automobile). The 1940's produced record incidences of extra-marital affairs and marital dissolutions, no doubt due to the social upheaval of the war. The 1960's was the time when the baby boom hit adolescence. They went a little further than the previous generations but the big difference was not how much further they went but that they bragged about it rather than trying to be discreet. In the past 15 years, there has been a small change (toward liberalization) in the way that people behave sexually, but a great change in the degree to which sexual behaviors are discussed in public. Most of these credos, however, would have been believed in 1960.

TEENAGERS

840

... that during adolescence, middle class kids succumb to lower class values; they become irresponsible and instinctual.

841

... that parents' attitudes on teenage sex depends upon whether they have sons or daughters.

842

... that chaperones are no longer utilized and today's young people would not pay attention to chaperones if they were there.

843

... that teenage males develop an awkwardly long gait which college or military corrects.

844

... that teenagers spend hours in the bathroom and most of this time is spent contemplating their complexions in a mirror.

845

... that adolescents engage in more fads than any other age group but it is better for them to get involved in a fad than sex, drugs, vandalism or political causes.

846

... that if three of the most popular girls in high school start wearing jingle bells on purple shoelaces, in less than a week all of the stores in town will be sold out of jingle bells and purple shoelaces.

847

... that when their kids run away from home, middle class parents hope that the kids will call up and beg to come back; that they will be healthy and safe, and that they have learned a good lesson.

Teenagers — Analysis

Adolescence is a most difficult time for those going through it and those around them. One reason for this is that it is a boring time of life. Childish games no longer satisfy and adult opportunities are not yet available. Most adolescent behavior can be understood as the attempt at aimless activity in order to displace the pervasive boredom. A second problem is that adolescents have very little status in our society, yet they have learned to be aware of the implications of status and crave it intensely. Therefore, they frequently behave like lower class people (840) until they can be assured that they will make it in the middle class. Usually, college or the first job is sufficient to do this. The quest for fads (845), vandalism and sexual experimentation must be seen as having a dual function: release from boredom and an attempt to get some status (or at least the feeling of being accepted or powerful).

During the 1960's, adolescents as a group had more status because a large percentage of the population was in that stage of the life cycle. Adolescent fashion and music became so popular that the older generation imitated or, at least, modified it. The extended adolescence of the baby boom generation is now over so there is less status in having such teenage affectations as a rebellious lifestyle or contemporary music, and more status in having such middle age affectations as a prestigious career, smart investments and an elegant residence.

TRANSPORTATION

848
... that middle class people feel like spendthrifts if they fly first class.

849
... that in order to find middle class people in true form, go to the airport; in order to find lower class people in true form, go to the bus station; the people hanging around the bus station without tickets are the lowest of the lower class.

850
... that years ago, private transit companies gave better service for a dime than public transit offers for a dollar today.

851
... that United States drivers, at least those outside of the large cities, are the world's most considerate.

852
... that new cars never get the estimated miles per gallon.

853
... that each year several inventors discover how to make a car get over 100 miles per gallon but the big oil companies suppress the idea.

854
... that the first gas station, restaurant or parking lot that has a sign saying "last chance" is probably lying.

855
... that middle class people never run out of gas or else prepare for the event by joining the triple A.

856

... that the 55 miles per hour speed limit is ridiculous on a straight, flat, empty, four-lane highway at 3:00 A.M.

857

... that if stoplights did not take so long to change, fewer people would try to run a yellow light.

858

... that cars which are old, large and brightly colored are driven by lower class people.

859

... that lower class people would rather spend money on making a car look good than run well.

860

... that lower class people are careless drivers and more frequently involved in auto accidents, but usually do not carry liability insurance.

861

... that middle class people regularly perform preventive maintenance on their cars and send their cars to garages for major repairs; lower class people work on their cars in the front yard so everyone else can see how mechanically inclined they are, and most of the repairs they make are major, due to the fact that they fail to perform preventative maintenance.

862

... that if all cars were invisible and silent, everyone would drive a Toyota.

863

... that the only people who go the wrong way on one-way streets are drunks and out-of-towners.

864

... that if seatbelts and infant car seats were easier to get in and out of, more people would use them.

865

... that the people who drive a car with a bumper sticker saying, "My other car is a Rolls Royce," are driving their best car.

... that taxi cabs are the most dented and dirtiest cars on the road.

867

... that the full-sized cars that Detroit is coming out with today are about as big as the compacts of a decade ago but cost four times as much.

868

... that a big car is safer because it is more visible and there is more metal around you.

869

... that a small car is safer because it is more maneuverable.

870

... that old cadillacs look like wrecks due to the fact that most of them are owned by lower class people; old Mercedes look elegant due to the fact that they are well maintained by their middle class owners.

871

... that when middle class people get more than two kids and a dog, they purchase a large station wagon; lower class men purchase vans, pickups and campers, not to carry their kids around but to escape from the family on weekends.

872

... that people believe that their old car is worth more than book value.

873

... that drivers more often give right-of-way to old, big cars due to the fact that the drivers figure that the old, big car would do more damage to their cars than vice versa.

874

... that traffic is worse today than it was 10 years ago.

875

... that traffic is worse on Friday afternoons, especially before a three day weekend.

876

... that left turns are the cause of much traffic congestion.

877

... that when you don't allow people to make a left turn, they just have to drive all the way around the block and try to get into the street from a different angle and this means more driving and more traffic, not to mention greater frustration.

878

... that half of the downtown traffic is due to people driving around looking for a parking place.

879

... that if more parking space were constructed downtown, more people would be encouraged to bring their cars and this would increase traffic.

880

... that there are too many parking places reserved for the handicapped.

881

... that there should be a system for getting wrecks off the street sooner and for sweeping up the broken glass.

882

... that up until a few years ago, people with four-wheel drive vehicles actually used them off the road.

Transportation — Analysis

There are so many credos about transportation because it is such a central aspect of middle class life, the bridge uniting residence and place of employment. The basic problem with American transportation is that the automobile has so many conveniences and status builders (862, 865) that individuals do not want to give it up, but it has so many disadvantages which we have not yet learned to overcome or tolerate. These latter factors account for the frustrations in transportation (856-857, 864), some of which appear in the form of paradoxes (876-879).

The other theme running through these credos is that lower class people and adolescents place special emphasis on the status potential of the car, and have emphasized its sight and sound factors (858-859, 870-871) to such an extent that bright and loud cars give the driver an adolescent/lower class status.

TELEVISION & RADIO

883

... that before television was invented, children spent their time doing chores and homework and participating in wholesome activities like the scouts.

884

... that the level and volume of music in TV drama is overdone.

885

... that the better the TV program, the more commercials they put on.

886

... that the TV networks take three good shows and put them in the same time slot to compete against each other.

887

... that the long pledge breaks on public TV are worse than commercials.

888

... that watching TV makes one lazy and is addictive.

889

... that from about 6:00 P.M. to 11:00 P.M., the water pressure in large cities gets dangerously low every half hour.

890

... that the only households without a TV are those in which the people live very interesting lives.

891

... that there were fewer hyperactive kids before TV.

... that of all the commercials, those for insect extermination are the most ridiculous, cleaning products are the most boring, pain relievers are the most obnoxious, pet food are the cutest.

... that special news bulletins never interrupt commercials or previews of coming attractions.

... that women newscasters have harsh nasal voices and they affect this intentionally in order to sound more masculine.

... that trivia talk shows are boring unless they talk about something you remember.

... that Johnny Carson takes more time off from his job than a government worker with unlimited sick leave.

... that authors and actors only go on talk shows to plug their forthcoming books and movies.

... that radio talk shows are interesting, but too many nuts call up.

Television & Radio — Analysis

The attitude on these media parallels the negative attitude toward contemporary movies, music and press. There is some nostalgia and the conviction that things are getting worse. Not only has TV failed to live up to its potential, but also there is the fear that it has an adverse impact on children and family life (888, 891).

Furthermore, the middle class sees itself neglected in programming. Most of the sitcoms are on such a low intellectual level so that lower class people and kids will watch them. There is PBS, but there are problems there (887) including the fact that much of the programming is so high brow that only literature professors and people with upper class affectations would bother to watch. The truly middle class programming is the news and the talk shows, which leave much to be desired (893-898).

VICES

899

... that no one enjoys the first cigarette.

900

... that middle class people smoke in order to cope with the stress that comes from trying to maintain a middle class existence; lower class people smoke in order to show off.

901

... that smoking is a dirty habit and not good for human health but there are worse things than smoking.

902

... that drunks do and say funny things only in jokes.

903

... that the liquid consumed out of those little brown bags in public parks and on skid row is wine.

904

... that alcohol has some medicinal purposes but the people who say that they use it for medicinal purposes are embarrassed by the fact that they like to drink.

905

... that alcoholics do not admit to being such but members of Alcoholics Anonymous continue to refer to themselves as alcoholics regardless of how many years they have been sober.

906

... that only lower class people and alcoholics drink before noon on weekdays.

. . . that few Jews, Italians or Orientals are alcoholics.

. . . that most drunks turned to alcohol because their lives were too stressful.

. . . that if middle class people drink, they lament the cost and try to buy liquor at a discount house, while lower class drinkers are more concerned with instant availability when they buy their liquor.

. . . that people go out of their way to avoid using the participle of the verb "to drink" unless they wish to convey intoxication.

. . . that smoking marijuana makes people hungry.

. . . that people high on alcohol are more dangerous than people high on marijuana.

. . . that gamblers and drinkers promise you they'll stop, but don't.

. . . that every horseplayer has a system which he swears by, but none of these systems work.

. . . that some blackjack players have a system that works, and have become very wealthy with it; so much so that some blackjack dealers in casinos have been trained to spot players who have a system and refuse to let them play.

Vices — Analysis

The middle class realizes that smoking is not smart, drunks are not cute (902), and gambling does not pay (914). There are serious mental/

physical health risks and pose family problems. Only the stress relieving and addictive characteristics of these habits perpetuate them. The lower class and adolescents fail to realize all of this and believe that these vices are the way to be sophisticated and powerful.

WAR

916
... that after wartime, the proportion of male births increases.

917
... that the United States should not get involved in any war that it cannot or will not win.

918
... that most of our "allies" would not rush to our defense if we were attacked.

919
... that most people do not know where a small country is until American troops are sent there.

920
... that Alexander and Napoleon were military geniuses.

921
... that U. S. Grant was a better general than president.

922
... that Custer was a poor military tactician.

923
... that Moslems believe that war is holy.

924
... that Germany could have won World War II if only they...

925
... that most World War II buffs have a secret admiration of Hitler.

926
... that any book on Germany or World War II will sell better if there is a large swastika on the cover.

927
... that on some tiny island in the Pacific, there is still a Japanese soldier who has not yet heard that the war is over.

928
... that if that soldier could see Tokyo and Detroit, he would never believe which side won the war.

929
... that every adult over 40 remembers not only the year but the date that United States involvement in World War II began and ended, but no one remembers when the United States involvement in Vietnam began or ended.

930
... that the number of people who claim to be absolute pacifists depends upon the war which happens to be going on.

931
... that the most intelligent people going into the service select the Navy or Air Force for the technical opportunities; the gutsiest guys go into the Marines; the Army takes what's left.

932
... that there will never be peace in the world as long as there is. . .

War – Analysis

Middle class people and Americans in general like peace but have accepted war and defense as a part of life (937). People who urge disarmament are either in adolescent naivete or else are communist sympatizers (309). No one, dove or hawk, wants another Vietnam (917). If and when a war does come, Americans hope that it will be a short, popular one that we can win without having to suffer too much.

WORK

933

... that everyone would like other people to believe that his job is more important than it is.

934

... that 50 years ago, children and adults had more work to do, therefore, less opportunity to get into trouble.

935

... that everybody wants to start at the top.

936

... that jobs which require a master's degree today did not require a college degree or even a high school diploma 50 years ago.

937

... that inefficient people gravitate toward government jobs; efficient and responsible people get very frustrated working for the government.

938

... that prostitutes earn several hundred dollars a day but squander it all on drugs and pimps.

940

... that those who can, do; those who can't do it, sell it; those who can't sell it, teach it; those who can't teach are teaching anyway due to tenure.

941

... that most men would rather be self-employed, or at least say they would, and the reason most men are not self-employed is that they are afraid of the financial insecurities and the loss of fringe benefits.

... that the person who is self-employed and working weekends resents the fact that he is not making any overtime.

... that the person who works for a large company and works late hours resents the fact that he is not sharing in any of the profits.

... that workers paid by the hour work slower.

... that lower class men make a career of the first job they get.

... that every man who works with his hands wishes that he had become a plumber or a truck driver.

... that lower class people view success as joining a strong union like the teamsters; middle class people view success as becoming a physician or getting an M.B.A. from Harvard or Stanford.

... that unions always ask for more than they expect to get.

... that when unions do not get as much as they want, they go on strike and issue a press statement accusing management of not bargaining in good faith.

... that American cars cannot compete with Japanese cars because the U.A.W. has won such a high level of wages and benefits for American workers.

... that unions cause inflationary spirals, paralyze the national economy with strikes and impede more efficient methods of production.

... that without unions all the gains made by labor in the past century would be wiped out.

953
. . . that an American worker cannot keep body and soul together while working at the minimum wage level.

954
. . . that Mexicans come to this country to work at wages often below the minimum wage so that they can raise their living standard and send money back home to their families.

955
. . . that illegal aliens make better domestic servants than Americans do.

956
. . . that janitors do not follow the written instructions left for them because they cannot read English.

957
. . . that after a three day weekend, it is hard to go back to work.

958
. . . that when American workers are finally given a four day work week, they will start striking for a three day work week.

959
. . . that the American Medical Association and American Bar Association are unions which refuse to admit that they are.

960
. . . that the United States would be better off with twice as many physicians and half as many lawyers.

961
. . . that 30 years ago, women went into nursing with the hope of marrying a doctor but this is no longer the case for only half of them are going into nursing in hopes of marrying a doctor.

962
. . . that women physicians are either the nicest ones you have ever met or else extremely defensive about their gender.

963
... that physicians have the most illegible handwriting.

964
... that only pharmacists can read physician's handwriting.

965
... that every pharmacists wishes that he could have studied medicine instead.

966
... that if people who have mental problems have enough intelligence and stick-to-it-tiveness to make it through a graduate program, they become psychologists.

967
... that with fluoride preventing so many cavities, dentistry is not nearly as lucrative as it used to be.

968
... that most job applicants exaggerate on their resumes.

969
... that it is best not to appear too eager or desperate when buying a home or car, or when applying for a job.

970
... that people who send out resumes with a letter asking for a job are desperate.

971
... that when companies are not hiring applicants, they usually send out nice letters saying that the resume will be kept on file for future needs, but do not save these resumes.

972
... that any job applicant who is late for an interview because of car trouble will not get the job.

973
... that if you go to a job interview and the secretary calls you by your first name, you are going to wait a long time.

... that most applicants cannot furnish the addresses of the companies that they previously worked for.

... that at night, on luxury liners, the crew has more fun than the passengers.

... that when college educated people wind up with menial jobs, they bad mouth the company, the government, the economic system, and try to get into radical politics or union leadership.

... that if you write a letter on company stationery, your boss will hear about it.

... that there is a lot of money to be made in. . .

... that most of the people who go into . . . do not make enough and are out within six months.

... that construction workers are very expert at blowing their noses without using handkerchiefs.

... that workaholics are pretty happy; they enjoy their work and few people spend as much of their lives doing something they enjoy.

... that the spouses of workaholics are unhappy with the little attention that they get from the workaholic but do not complain about the workaholic's economic rewards.

... that the firms which give gold watches at retirement dinners usually underpay their workers.

... that working class men do not feel good about the wife working and they feel especially bad if their wives have a better job than they do.

... that two-career marriages suffer additional strains, especially when both careers require geographic mobility.

... that accountants are quiet and responsible, except for the one that you know.

... that most adult welfare recipients could get a job if they had to.

... that a responsible, mature, working man feels personally guilty about being laid off in a period of economic downturn.

... that people who get fired refuse to accept responsibility for it and accuse the boss of having it in for them.

... that if you do not like your boss, it is because he or she has already reached a level of incompetence.

... that assembly line workers have the most boring jobs.

... that men who wear keyrings on the outside of their pants are lower class but trying to impress everyone with how much responsibility they have at work; middle class people who want to show off how important their work is carry briefcases or wear beepers.

... that the people who occupy the corner offices are the most important.

... that the most stressful work is the mental exertion of highly paid executives sitting on plush chairs in air-conditioned offices with a penthouse view.

995

... that people who never talk about their jobs never do anything interesting at work.

996

... that people who never talk about their jobs must be doing something top secret or very complicated.

997

... that no one's job is ever perfectly adjusted to one's abilities, either the job is too routine, easy and insufficiently challenging, or else it is too stressful and draining.

Work — Analysis

There are more credos on this topic than any other. Careers are such an important topic today because the baby boom generation is in its 30's, the decade which offers the best opportunity for advancing in a career and the last clear chance for major career change. A person's occupation offers three important things: pay, fulfillment, and status. Each worker feels underpaid (942-943). Everyone feels that career offers insufficient fulfillment (997) but some people are quite pleased (981).

Occupation may be the most important index of social class (Lundberg, 1974). Each occupation carries a certain degree of prestige (Treiman, 1977; 933, 935, 992), and there are key differences between lower class "jobs" and middle class "careers." The former involve the manipulation of objects and are more inclined to be directly supervised, while the latter are more likely to involve the manipulation of ideas, symbols and human relations and permit more self-direction (Kohn, 1969). While middle class occupations provide more opportunities to advance on the basis of ability and effort, this is less likely with lower class positions and so the interest in labor unions (947).

.

CONCLUSION

998

... that every reader was offended by some of these credos.

999

... that anyone who agrees with less than 50 percent of these statements is not true, red-white-and-blue, American middle class.

1000

... that anyone who agrees with more than 90% of these statements is not true, red-white-and-blue, American middle class, but is trying very hard to camouflage the fact.

Conclusion — Analysis

In the revised version of his credos, Nathan's (1927) last credo was that the average American did not believe most of them. Nathan was probably right for two reasons. First, many of his credos were superstitions that most Americans had heard of but did not acknowledge. Second, Nathan himself led a true upper class existence as a newspaper drama critic and many of his credos reflected that experience and were quite alien to most middle class Americans.

Because Americans are so opinionated (564), it would be impossible to come up with a list of credos that could get more than 90% agreement (1000). Nevertheless, if Americans will read these thousand statements and respond without reflection, I am confident that middle class Americans will find themselves agreeing with most of them (999); well, anyway, that is my credo.

Middle class Americans are disgusted with movies, music, television, radio, salesmen, products, politics and the press. They are perplexed by transportation, bureaucratic and economic problems. They are not getting enough prestige, let alone satisfaction, out of marriage, residence or career.

Middle class Americans believe (and hope) that they will find happiness with a new job, larger home in a better neighborhood, warmer interpersonal relationship, or maybe just a hundred dollars more discretionary income a month; but their intrinsic striving for something better makes it impossible for them to be satisfied at any level. However, one thing is certain, the American middle class would trade places neither with foreign nobility nor its lower class compatriots.

Will class differences diminish in the American future? Despite the government's feeble attempt to equalize the wealth and opportunity, I predict that social class differences will increase throughout the remainder of this century, due to an interaction of childrearing, educational and occupational variables. In five years, there will be two distinct classes of children in school: those with younger, lower class mothers, and those with older, middle class mothers (429). The latter group, fearing the failure of public education, will have so over-prepared their kids that there will be a bumper crop of super-geniuses among them. When their middle class parents hear of this fact, they will foresee the competition to get into medical school in 2002 A.D., and push their kids even harder to be overachievers and thus fully inculcate the Middle Class Credo. Even those kids who do not get into medicine will be primed for careers of leadership in a technological society: business, engineering, human relations, etc. On the other hand, lower class mothers, who are themselved ill-prepared for the world of the 1980's, will transmit these feelings to their offspring: futility and hostility. When these kids, who have only been prepared for technological society by virtue of hours in front of TV's and video games, come to grips with the numerical and verbal fundamentals in school, they will not grasp them. When they see the great ability of the middle class geniuses, a feeling of inferiority will develop and then increase the feelings of futility and hostility. Many of these lower class children will be permanently unemployable or else have to compete fiercely for the few menial jobs that cybernation does not do away with.

APPENDIX ON METHOD

Many psychologists and sociologists will be curious about the methodology by which these data were accumulated. This method is a synthesis of sociology's participant observation and psychology's introspection. Participant observation research is characterized by a period of intense interaction between the observer and the usual participants in the social system being investigated. The goal is to collect data in such a way that is both unobstrusive and systematic (Bogdan & Taylor, 1975). Some example's of this technique would be Lynd's (1929) study of a small town and Gans' (1967) study of a suburban housing development. Since all Americans are enmeshed in the social class system to one degree or another, the method of participant observation may be particularly appropriate here.

While participant observation is in vogue in sociology, introspection has not been a major research tool in psychology for 50 years. Titchener (1909) distinguished between external observations (inspection: looking at) and internal observations (introspection: looking within) of the observations of one's own mind in an effort to discover the laws that govern the mind. Introspection was one way of studying thought and emotion as subjectively perceived. Titchener (1909) also suggested that sociology could be introspective discipline because it studied institutions such as customs, law, religion, myth and speech, which were the results of introspections made in common by members of a social group.

The pressure of the behaviorists, who contended that introspective data were contaminated by subjective factors, led to gradual abandonment of this method in scientific psychology, though it survived in clinical psychoanalysis as free association (Boring, 1959b). It is true that introspective data are vulnerable to distortion because the subject must break the stream of consciousness in order to remember and report the stream (Boring, 1959a). In this way, the process of introspective inevitably distorts its products.

However, introspection can give us some information about experience, some data otherwise unobtainable. As with all research methods, it has certain limitations which must be realized and certain risks which must be guarded against (Radford, 1974). Titchener (1909) was well aware of the problems inherent in breaking the stream of consciousness in order to report it. His remedy was to allow the stream to continue as long as it was fruitful and then later use retrospection in an attempt to recover the thought. His guidelines also included a call for objectivity, by which he implied facing facts as they come without trying to edit or force them into a prefabricated theory, and working only when the disposition was favorable.

The sociological technique of participant observation has been used extensively in the past decade and so it has also developed some guidelines for overcoming the problems of qualitative research. The key is quite similar to Titchener's ideas: maintaining a balanced alternation between being a participant in the social system and being the observer of that system: being able both to identify with the other participants and to detach oneself from this involvement when an objective reporting becomes necessary (Bogdan & Taylor, 1975). In other words, one must simultaneously avoid both the extreme of aversion and the extreme of over-identification (Bollens & Marshall, 1973).

The present study took place over a seven year period as the author lived in various neighborhoods: lower class Black in Chicago, lower class integrated in Chicago, lower class integrated in California, and then the last four years in San Carlos. This compact city of 25,000 is nestled between the coastal mountains and the San Francisco Bay. The outstanding points of San Carlos are low crime rate, a small town atmosphere provided by a central business district rather than shopping centers, excellent climate (away from San Francisco fog and San Jose smog), and a half hour commute to just about anywhere in the Bay Area. Many new families moving in are dual career, not only because of the necessary income level for meeting rents or mortgage payments, but also because the location is ideal if one spouse works in the city and the other works in Silicon Valley. Homeowners who purchased prior to 1974 were middle class (some working class). Newer residents are high income purchasers and middle class renters, except for a small area by the railroad track. Here, the author purchased a cement block home in 1977. New owner-occupants in this neighborhood are middle class but at least half the homes are held by speculators who rent them out to younger, working class tenants. There are few truly lower class people in San Carlos due to the lack of services for them, but many of these renters down by the railroad tracks exhibit some classic lower class behavior.

The author also listened to radio talk shows and observed neighbors of both social classes. The credos were recorded when the author became cognizant of them. Many times this came in casual conversation or on a radio talk show, but frequently the author observed behavior, empathized with the participants (Weber, 1968; Bogdan & Taylor, 1975) and then introspected to find the cognitive and affective components consistent with the observed behavioral component of the attitude. Data were later checked by searching for similar statements in popular publications, talk shows or casual conversations. A total of over 1600 aphorisms were thus collected and those that were least representative or verifiable were discarded along with those that were essential duplicates.

It might be asked if this method is sufficiently scientific and why it should be preferred to the quantifiable data generated by a questionnaire. That which separates psychology and sociology from philosophical speculations and gives them scientific status is the possibility of performing primary induction (Kneale, 1959). These credos were recorded individually and only later, when there was an attempt to categorize them, was it noticed that social class was such a pervasive theme. There is the risk that the observer's specific environment or social consciousness was not representative, that it was or became peculiarly obsessed with issues of social class. The previously mentioned guidelines for participant observation and introspection were used to minimize this very real risk.

Could objectivity have been better preserved by a questionnaire which asked a sample of middle class subjects to register agreement or disagreement with a list of statements? Both qualitative and quantitative methodologies make some assumptions about translating subjective experience into data but the assumptions are different. A questionnaire assumes that the subject will answer in such a way as to accurately indicate those maxims upon which everyday life is based. Demand effect and improper wording of questions can make that assumption untenable (Rosenthal, 1976). This was one reason why the author chose to passively observe the credos as they were expressed and observe the behavior based on the credos.

Another factor which was very potent in the initial stages of this project was to replicate the methodology of Nathan and Mencken (1921). They had similarly opted for a qualitative, intuitive approach after declaring the limitations of the experimental method in social psychology. Nathan (1927) later expressed contentment with the favorable scholarly reaction to this method. The anti-quantitative approach was later championed by Sorokin (1956) and Phillips (1973). Bogdan and Taylor (1975) attempted to put things into perspective by noting that sociology has long had both positivist and phenomenological tendencies. The former has ignored the subjective states in an effort to get quantifiable data and the latter has distrusted quantifiable data because they ignore subject states. I contend that social class, unlike mass and electric charge, exists primarily in the perceptions of persons and the study of social class must have a phenomenological dimension which is both logically and chronologically prior to any attempt at quantification.

REFERENCES

Adler, A. *The individual psychology of Alfred Adler*. NY: Harper & Row, 1956.

Banfield, E.C. *The unheavenly city revisited*. Boston: Little, Brown & Co., 1974.

Bloom, R. D., Whiteman, M. & Deutsch, M. Race and social class as separate factors. In *The Disadvantaged Child*, M. Deutsch, ed. NY: Basic, 1967.

Bogdan, R. & Taylor, S. J. *Introduction to qualitative research methods*. NY: Wiley, 1975.

Bollens, J. C. & Marshall, D. R. *A guide to participation: field work role playing cases and other forms*. Englewood Cliffs, NJ: Prentice-Hall, 1973.

Boring, E. G. Consciousness. *Encyclopedia Britannica*, 1959a, 6, 283-284.

Boring, E. G. Introspection. *Encyclopedia Britannica*, 1959b, 12, 542.

Brink, G. S. & Brink, T. L. Manifest dream content of undocumented Mexican immigrants. *Interamerican Journal of Psychology* 1978, 12, 137-141.

Coleman, R.P. & Rainwater, L. *Social standing in America: new dimensions of class*. NY: Basic, 1978.

DeToqueville, A. *Democracy in America*. NY: Harper & Row, 1966.

Dickson, P. *The official explanations*. NY: Delacorte, 1980.

Gans, H.J. *The Levittowners: ways of life and politics in a new suburban community*. NY: Pantheon, 1967.

Kneale, W.C. Scientific method. *Encyclopedia Britannica*, 1959, 20, 127-130.

Kohn, M.L. Social class and parent-child relationships. *American Journal of Sociology*, 1963, 68, 471-480.

Kohn, M.L. *Class and conformity: a study in values*. Homewood: Dorsey Press, 1969.

Lundberg, M.J. *The incomplete adult: social class constraints in personality development*. Westport, Conn.: Greenwood Press, 1974.

Lynd, R.S. *Middletown: a study in contemporary American culture*. NY: Harcourt, Brace & Co., 1929.

Mintzberg, H. *The structure of organizations*. Englewood Cliffs, NJ: Prentice-Hall, 1979.

Nathan, G.J. *The new American credo: a contribution toward the interpretation of the national mind*. NY: Knopf, 1927.

Nathan, G.J. & Mencken, H.L. *The American credo: a contribution toward the study of the American mind*. NY: Knopf, 1921.

Packard, V. *The status seekers*. NY: David McKay, 1959.

Phillips, D.L. *Abandoning method*. San Francisco: Jossey-Bass, 1973.

Radford, J. Reflections on introspection. *American Psychologist*, 1974, 29, 245-250.

Rosenthal, R. *Experimenter effects in behavioral research*. NY: Wiley, 1976.

Rothman, R.A. *Inequality and social stratification in the U.S.* Englewood Cliffs, NJ: Prentice-Hall, 1978.

Shils, E.A. Class. *Encyclopedia Britannica*, 1959, 5, 768-768B.

Sorokin, P.A. *Fads and foibles in modern sociology and related sciences*. Chicago: Regnery, 1956.

Tillich, P. *Systematic theology*. Chicago: University of Chicago Press, 1951.

Titchener, E.B. *A Textbook of psychology*. NY: MacMillan, 1909.

Treiman, D. *Occupational prestige in comparative perspective*. NY: Academic, 1977.

Veblen, T.B. *The theory of the leisure class: an economic study of institutions*. NY: MacMillan, 1899.

Weber, M. *Economy and society: an outline of interpretive sociology*. NY: Bedminster, 1968.

ABOUT THE AUTHOR

Dr. Brink had undergraduate majors in history and religious studies before obtaining a teaching credential, an M.B.A., and a doctorate in psychology. He serves as a consultant to mental health agencies (on againg) and to high technology industry (on the recruitment of engineers and managers). He has been on the faculties of the College of Notre Dame, Palo Alto School of Professional Psychology and Stanford Medical School. He has authored over 50 journal articles, eleven encyclopedia articles and a previous book on aging and mental health.